15~
Architect?
7/20

Islamic Architecture

OTTOMAN TU

D0129172

Scorpion Publications Limited

© Text: Godfrey Goodwin 1977

All rights reserved. No part of this publication may
be reproduced, stored in a retrieval system, or
transmitted in any form or by any means, electronic,
mechanical, photocopying, recording or otherwise,
without the prior permission of the copyright owner.

First published 1977 by
Scorpion Publications Limited
PO Box No 1 London WC2E
ISBN 0 905906 02 0

Managing Editor: Antony Hutt
Series Editor: Leonard Harrow
Design and Art Direction: Colin Larkin
Design Assistant: Rhonda Larkin
Photographic: Antony Hutt, Warwick Ball, John Warren,
Julian Raby and Steven Crane

Set in Monophoto Ehrhardt 453 and 573
Printed on Blade Coated Matt Art 081/120 gsm
Originated, filmset, printed and bound by
Westerham Press Ltd Westerham Kent

Contents

Acknowledgements

The author would like to acknowledge the use of photographs by the Artomonov Collection, Freer Gallery of Art, Washington, Michael Stewart Thompson, the Turkish Ministry of Tourism, the Hon. R. R. E. Chorley, Warwick Ball, Julian Raby and Antony Hutt.

List of Illustrations

Series Note

This volume forms part of an extensive series of illustrated and introductory works covering most aspects of Islamic art and architecture. While these books will serve as a source of reference for the serious student, they are also intended to provide more general information for the average reader.

Note on Spelling

Technical terms and proper names are spelt in
in this volume according to modern romanised
Turkish spelling.

The Ottoman Empire

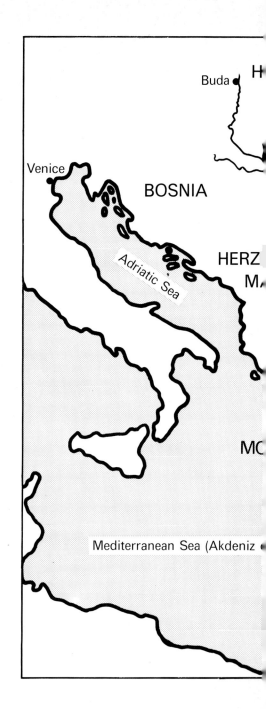

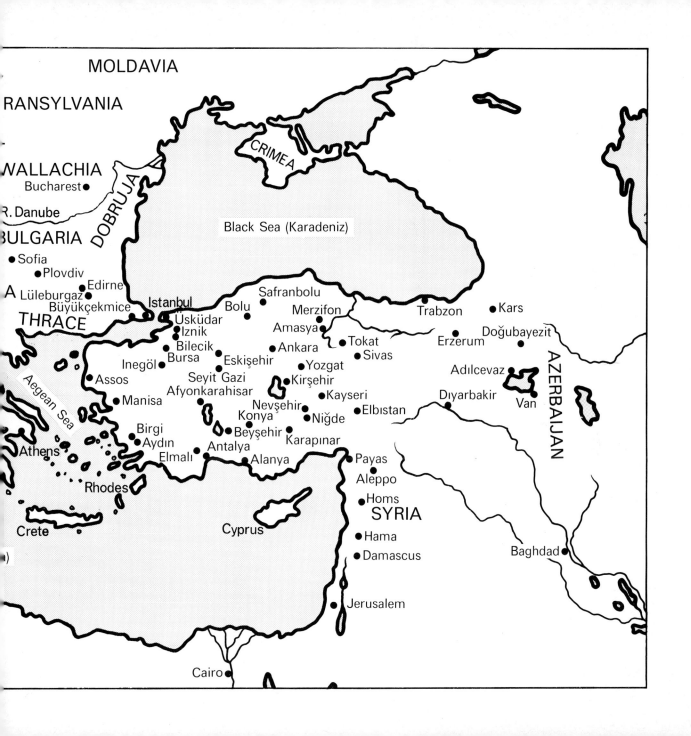

MOLDAVIA

RANSYLVANIA

WALLACHIA
Bucharest

R. Danube

BULGARIA
Sofia
Plovdiv
Lüleburgaz Edirne
Büyükçekmice
THRACE

DOBRUJA

CRIMEA

Black Sea (Karadeniz)

Istanbul
Üsküdar
Iznik
Bilecik
Inegöl
Bursa
Assos

Aegean Sea

Manisa

Birgi
Aydın
Athens
Elmalı

Rhodes

Crete

Safranbolu
Bolu
Merzifon
Amasya
Ankara
Eskişehir
Seyit Gazi
Afyonkarahisar
Konya
Beyşehir
Antalya
Alanya

Trabzon
Kars
Doğubayezit
Erzerum

Tokat
Sivas
Yozgat
Kirşehir
Nevşehir
Kayseri
Niğde
Elbıstan
Karapınar

Adılcevaz
Van
Diyarbakir

AZERBAIJAN

Payas
Aleppo
Homs
SYRIA
Hama
Damascus

Cyprus

Baghdad

Jerusalem

Cairo

To Bertie

Introduction

The Early Period

The early Ottoman chieftains were soldiers whose palace was their tent yet their tombs were often larger than their mosques, like the converted chapel in which Osman himself was buried, while the reconstructed mosque of Ertuğrul, his father, at Söğüt is a room in which some twenty men might make their genuflexions. It was a meeting-place for brother warriors pledged to advance the frontiers of Islam. These captains of small bands included Byzantine adventurers attracted to the service of a dynamic, upstart family. Even when Yıldırım Beyazit, the Thunderbolt, was defeated by Timur in 1402 the Ottoman dynasty survived fratricidal strife and within fifty years Mehmet II, the Conqueror, had recovered the lost territories, taken Constantinople and reached Belgrade.

Until the mystic Murat II sought seclusion, the Ottomans walked among their people. Murat's son, Mehmet II, was walled in by his absolute authority but still any free subject could petition his stirrup when he rode through his city. In the 16th century Süleyman the Lawgiver, known in the west as the Magnificent, divided his overwhelming temporal power. The Greek slave, Ibrahim Pasha, who had been his boyhood companion, became the first Grand Vizir. By then the square hall under a hemispherical dome flanked by a slender minaret was the insignia of the Ottoman presence from the Danube to the Indian Ocean. Two hundred years before, the family had had to invent an ancestry and Ertuğrul and Osman were more concerned with flocks than subjects.

It was Orhan I who established the dynasty and built a substantial mosque at Bilecik with a watch tower for a minaret on the commanding height above its own escarpment. At Iznik little chapels developed into such handsome monuments as the

Green Mosque with its subtle double-square plan, ornate portico and intricate plasterwork.

The conquest of Bursa brought Orhan the revenues of a great market with which to finance a rapid expansion of power. There beside the bazaar he built a royal mosque which combined a chapel with a *zaviye* or hostel for *dervishes*. The plan was perfected with the complex of Yıldırım Beyazit, set on a spur of Uludağ or Mount Olympus, and reached its climax with the richly tiled Green Mosque of Mehmet I.

These royal foundations were copied by the vizirs and senior officers. Preceded by a spacious porch for latecomers to prayer, and also for relaxation and gossip, a vestibule leads into an inner court under the major dome with an oculus which permitted water to refresh the central pool. On each side are recesses or *iwans* for meditation and retiring rooms with plaster shelves for jugs and flowers. As a rule, each unit was domed as was the mosque hall which was raised two or three steps above the courtyard. Thus a number of cupolas clustered round the central court dome. At the Green Mosque the dome of the prayer hall achieved equality of diameter with that of the court while at Beyazit II's foundation at Amasya, court and lateral rooms opened up to form an integral part of the mosque. Its hostel like its college was a separate building but the area before the *mihrab* continued to be raised a few centimetres higher and so set apart.

In the fourteenth and fifteenth centuries, the Bursa type of mosque was the grandest expression of Ottoman power. Some were built even after the fall of Constantinople including that of Rum Mehmet Pasha at Üsküdar. This mosque is interesting because of the Byzantine training of its Greek architect which resulted in a dome set on a brick drum, its rim undulating over windows, and an apse projecting under a half-dome. Elsewhere the Ottomans successfully enforced their own style on their Christian craftsmen although they adopted the apsidal form already embryonic in the projecting prayer halls of Bursa-type mosques.

Dervish rooms derived from the lodges of the Ahi brotherhood which had heterodox Sufi leanings. Fourteenth century travellers refer to Ahi hospitality and leadership even in towns where a prince resided. The Ottomans eradicated these socialist guildsmen since the spread of peaceful dominions requiring no frontiersmen strengthened the central government and an orthodox Sunni judiciary, the *Ulema*, jealous of heretical sects. This wholly conservative force was trained in religious and legal colleges or *medreses*. Orhan's brother, Süleyman Pasha, built the first Ottoman example at Iznik with a fountain court enclosed on three sides by student cells and their portico.

Colleges and Courtyards

The next college surmounted the mosque-zaviye of Orhan's heir, Murat I Hüdavendigâr, or the Prince. The cells of this unique example open onto galleries overlooking the inner court while a broad terrace, commanding magnificent views, extends over the portico. A Karaman prince built a similar terrace for his two-storey medrese at Niğde. The feature reflects the influence of the Adriatic littoral. Vizirial mosques and their colleges shared the same precinct. There could be no central entry to the complex because the lecture hall, if only for reasons of symmetry, was usually placed in the middle of the main block just where the grand portal ought to be. One solution to the problem was to enhance the importance of the side entrances while at Inegöl the mosque of Ishak Pasha was set twenty metres back from its college, although the fountain remained central to both, and thus any tensions were relaxed and dispersed.

Not until Sinan built the mosque of Sokollu Mehmet Pasha in Istanbul was an ideal answer found. This complex is situated on a hillside and hillsides inspired interesting variations in standard plans. The central entry forms a broad stair which ascends the hill with the lecture hall built over its tunnel-vault and approached by wing stairways. Thus the entrance is aligned with the mihrab and the hall enhances its grandeur.

Brilliance at Bursa

Royal foundations escaped the problem by setting their college apart with a separate quadrangle. Mosque forecourts did not develop until that of Üç Şerefeli built by Murat II but otherwise royal foundations were decently adorned. At the Green Mosque in Bursa lavishly carved marble is matched by panels of square green tiles, their pigment overset with shadows that add depth and overglazed with gold filigree, foils for sumptuous arabesque, polychrome medallions. The renowned mihrabs of mosque and tomb are triumphal gateways enveloped in glazed brick mosaic in the Timurid manner. These ceramics are the work of potters who were refugees from Mongol rule in Tabriz, Iran. They later went to Edirne to work on the mosques of Üç Şerefeli and Murat II's foundation in a suburb which was tended by dervishes of the Mevlevi order.

Set significantly on high, the Green Tomb or *türbe* relates to Seljuk antecedents both architecturally and in its veneration of forebears. Later examples were smaller but the domed octagon was the common form.

The first *beys* or barons ruled villages but Bursa was a prosperous city. The Moslem population was swelled by indigenous converts and newcomers seeking their fortune. To accommodate the large congregations the domed units multiplied. The Sehadet mosque, built in 1365, set one dome behind another to achieve a nave while that of Abdal Mehmet Bey had its twin units placed side by side which meant that there could be no central door. Both of these developments were overshadowed by the Great Mosque or Ulu Cami above the bazaar quarter. This first congregational mosque of the Ottomans was the work of Yıldırım Beyazit although Timur added the north portal. The original minaret stood at the north-west corner of the building which became the standard position. Earlier, minarets had been erected wherever was most convenient. Mehmet I added a second minaret and established the precedent that only a sultan's mosque might have more than one.

Surprisingly, the twenty domes in ranks of four by five achieve an interrelated interior space. Under the central dome in the second rank the large pool is all that remains of the inner court but the mihrab area which contains a noble walnut *minber* embossed with heavenly bodies is still contained beneath a single dome. The legend that Beyazit promised to build twenty mosques if God gave him the victory at Nicopolis, but afterwards economized by combining them in one, nicely exemplifies the early Ottoman concept of space.

The first Great Mosque in Edirne, renamed the Eski or Old Mosque after the building of a successor, has nine large domed units and a stalwart minaret with two balconies added as a consolation for its relegation to second place by Murat II's monument in a new style. Multidomed mosques continued to be built but by 1450 the form was archaic.

The Great Mosque and the Old Mosque have giant inscriptions on their walls and piers which may replace original work of similar magnitude. Highly formalized calligraphy was the universal decoration of mosques from the carved eulogy of the founder over the entry to the Qur'anic references to God as Light in the centre of the dome. Other quotations acquired established stations except in such mosques as that of Şehzade Mehmet where they were replaced by references to mortality for it was built out of Süleyman's grief at the death of his favourite son.

Calligraphy also decorated tiles, particularly in the lunette above a casement, mostly in an elegant and lofty script but at the Anatolian mosques of Ömer Pasha and Lala Mustafa Pasha the panels are crowded with a smaller hand.

Interlacing letters formed elaborate wheels or sun discs. Recent examples decorate the royal mosques of Bursa. These great circles are foils to the cubes of the open cross plan with its four corner rooms. This derived from Seljuk Persia and Greater Syria where the open courts were vast in comparison to those of the Ottomans which had to contract in order to support a dome. This central dome had inevitable significance because it was the grandest.

Palaces and Homes

It was a plan used for the palaces and sumptuous tents of Timur. Nothing remains of the modest wooden dwellings of the Ottoman beys at Bursa but they were probably related to the apartments in the Green Mosque. There the loge is flanked by withdrawing rooms which are entered from a loggia overlooking the plain. No comparison can be made with the vainglorious desert palaces of the Umayyads until Murat II built a substantial residence at Manisa which was destroyed by bandits in the 17th century. And since the pavilions in the pleasure grounds at Edirne were destroyed in the last century, the Çinili Kiosk built in the Timurid manner by Mehmet II in Istanbul is the earliest surviving Ottoman royal mansion.

The portico, rebuilt after a fire in the eighteenth century, admits to the state apartments over the less lofty vizirial rooms which are reached by a wide stair hidden under a trapdoor. In the basement are kitchens, wells and storerooms and access to a deep cellar or icehouse. Servants gained admittance by steps cut in the sills of tunnel-vaulted windows. The central hall beyond the vestibule leads to a projecting gazebo while on each side it opens onto lofty loggias. Like Nero in the Domus Aurea or Akbar at Fatihpur Sikri, Mehmet the Conqueror sat under the vault of heaven at the centre of the universe, the shadow of God on earth: but only the shadow. The private apartments overlooked the park and were embellished with dark tiles. The offices faced the terrace which was covered in glazed bricks and served as a grandstand from which the sultan could watch his courtiers and pages at sport.

At the palace of the Gun Gate – Topkapısaray – the royal tent fathered stone kiosks in parterres yet the cross plan is still discernible in the design of the main examples. The rest of the palace is a village of clearly defined service areas and the halls of the College of Pages. Once the function of each quarter is understood from the kitchens to the department of the Mistress of the Robes the sequence of courts and chambers is simple to follow. The cross plan dominated domestic as well as royal buildings especially the *yalıs* or mansions on the shores of the Bosphorus and the *konaks* of magnates in every town of the empire from the eighteenth century onwards. Even such uncompromisingly westernized palaces as that at Beylerbey or Dolmabahçe incorporated the formula.

The Çakır Bey Konak at Birgi is a good example of a lordly dwelling in the provinces. It preserves three sides of the cross plan with a bower projecting at third floor level where the owner sat in state at the centre of his household. Chambers in such mansions had foyers for servants and large closets concealing washing facilities and bedding. A step led up to the railed-off salon with its many casements and shelves for ewers and flowers. As with mosques the lower casements were for ventilation and had shutters against the winds of Anatolia while the sealed upper windows were for light and glazed, sometimes with coloured glass imported from Venice or Danzig.

Smaller town houses fitted cunningly into awkward sites. The ground floor kitchen and storerooms reflected the irregularities of the plot but the upper chambers and the broad verandah for family living projected over the street and courtyard in order to achieve rooms as rectangular as possible. This resulted in vistas of cantilevered rooms jostling down the street. Foundations and lower storeys were of brick and stone, indeed any old ruin or wall might be taken for this purpose, but upper floors were of timber with brick or wattle and daub infill in the interstices.

A courtyard was essential and most of the cooking was done in it. If possible it overflowed into a garden which was thus an extension of the house: during the Tulip Period the flowers retaliated and invaded the halls of the palace. Trees were loved and a great tree formed the heart of a village or neighbourhood and was a part of its architecture. Rags flying in the wind over the graves of holy men buried in state beneath such a tree turn it into a shamanist chapel-of-ease.

The flat-roofed crofts of the peasants and the poor had but one room and a byre. Then indeed the towns were dominated by monuments to God as is Edirne still when viewed across the river from Greece.

Towards the Semi-Dome

If Ottoman architecture were limited to the domed unit, the mosque of Selim I in Istanbul would have been its climax. Like the Beyazit complex at Edirne, hostels formed wings overshadowed by the prayer hall which was crowned with a dome as vast as engineering experience permitted. Inevitably the great church of Hagia Sophia challenged this limited concept. The great Umayyad mosque at Damascus had presented an earlier challenge. Its plan had penetrated southern Anatolia in Seljuk times. At its simplest it consisted of a central mihrab axis with one or two domes flanked by two or three long wing aisles. Such a mosque had little depth but the north wall opened to let the congregation overflow into the equally broad and narrow courtyard but the harsh winters of the central plateau precluded such an arrangement in Turkey. When Mongol power withered away, independent beys divided Anatolia between themselves. The rulers of Aydın modified the Damascus plan when Isa Bey erected a mosque near the ruined church of St. John at Ephesus. Its columns and revetments were quarried and its undercroft served as the pattern for the vaults under the mosque facade. The twin-domed mihrab axis opened onto the courtyard with two aisles extending on either side. The minarets are somewhat clumsily incorporated into the upper and lower side entrances for the mosque is built on the slope of a hill and has no central gateway.

After conquering the *beylik*, the Ottomans adapted the plan for the relatively small Güzelce Hasan Bey mosque at Hayrabolu in Thrace. This has a ten metre central dome with pairs of small domes on each side like the later Hatuniye and Valide mosques at Manisa. This is the ultimate Ottoman refinement of the Damascus plan and was the model for the new great mosque at nearby Edirne, the Üç Şerefeli Cami, with a dome 24 metres in diameter. Without stabilizing turrets, Ottoman engineers could build no greater.

These turrets appear at Beyazit II's mosque in Istanbul. Like pinnacles of flying buttresses, their weight anchors the supporting piers else the thrusts of the dome would buckle them. At the Mihrimah mosque Sinan was to use four turrets so massive that he could cut into the piers beneath at lower level without endangering their stability. Later mosques had eight piers and turrets which then could be halved in size and so gain in elegance. The dome of Üç Şerefeli mosque was supported outside by typical miniature flying buttresses and inside was borne on buttresses in the thickness of the walls and by two free-standing hexagonal piers nearly 5 metres thick. These divide the central area firmly from the wings where the shadowy extension of space adds to the grandeur of a sombre hall. The broad courtyard is the first monumental Ottoman example and has a fountain without a canopy. Just as Ibrahim I caged in the royal loges in the seventeenth century so Murat IV domed fountains with the result that the courtyards of Şehzade or Beyazit mosques in Istanbul appear cramped.

The Conqueror made Hagia Sophia his chief mosque but Ottoman builders studied it with caution. Mehmet employed Atık (the Venerable) Sinan, possibly the Greek Christodoulos, to build his university in Istanbul. The mosque had a single half-dome over the mihrab area so that the thrusts of the great dome were not equalized and the building was already unstable when the earthquake of 1766 brought it down. A smaller version of the Fatih mosque was built in Konya and gives an impression of the bulk of Atık Sinan's monument. Aesthetically, it must have compared badly with Hagia Sophia although the courtyard, which survived the earthquake, is handsome. It is not surprising that there is a legend that Mehmet II executed his architect.

When Beyazit II built his mosque in Istanbul a second half-dome was juxtaposed to that over the mihrab and heavy buttresses acted as extensions of the central supporting piers but this dome also collapsed in 1766.

It was not in Istanbul but in Elbistan and later Diyarbakır that four half-domes, the ideal support for a central dome, were introduced. The final form incorporating the exedras or subdomes employed at Hagia Sophia was achieved by Sinan at the mosque of Şehzade which is at once more logical and less mysterious than the Great Church. The monotony of the square ground plan is relieved by the north buttresses which are contained within the mosque, else they would deform the portico, whereas those supporting the mihrab wall, which had to be flat, are placed outside. The lateral buttresses are half inside and half out where they are masked within arcades. This concept was developed by Sinan at the subsequent Süleymaniye mosque where he sought to modify the monotony of unrelieved centralization. There the aisles have a rhythm of their own under cupolas of varying diameter and the two-tier lateral galleries are expressed inside as well as out thus relating exterior and interior in a manner that he was to perfect with the Selimiye mosque at Edirne.

The Great Mosques

Moreover, at Süleymaniye the flanking arcades are translated into facades, for mosque forecourts preclude any equivalent of the concept of a West Front. The grand entry to the courtyard, however, created insoluble problems which enforced the mutilation of capitals where the heights of columns varied because Ottoman architects rarely masked structural truth. Sinan did not repeat the mistake at Selim II's mosque where the gate does not obtrude.

He crowned this mosque with a dome 31 metres in diameter borne on eight piers. The magical interior space flows round the pivot of a central tribune erected above a fountain and into the side galleries which spread out over the exterior arcades to add a new dimension to the circumscribed expanse.

The Selimiye overwhelms its dependencies so that it is easy to overlook their extent. Such complexes began with the Bursa mosques which not only incorporated retreats but supported schools and hospitals. They were irregularly grouped because they were built on spurs of Uludağ. In Istanbul, Atık Sinan could set the Fatih mosque in the centre of a vast esplanade bounded by eight colleges, and their preparatory annexes, hospital, bath and hostel. Beyazit II's complex facing the river at Amasya was equally cohesive as was his extensive medical foundation at Edirne.

These achievements were surpassed by the university of Süleyman I above the Horn where over 500 domes were marshalled about the mosque. Its piazza and lawns were spacious yet space was never wasted and shops and taverns filled the vaults that support the huge platform on which the colleges, kitchens, asylum and hostel were built: except on the east side where two colleges descend the hill step by step so as not to mask the incomparable view of the mosques and royal tombs from the water.

Iznik Tiles, Paint and Glass

As opposed to the *cuerda seca* tiles at Fatih and the Şehzade tomb, Iznik underglaze tiles were introduced at Süleymaniye. An overwhelming display followed at the mosque of the dying Grand Vizir Rüstem Pasha but at that of Sokollu Mehmet Pasha, apart from the lunettes, they were concentrated on the minber hood and in one incomparable cascade down the lofty mihrab wall. In the Selimiye they fill the royal loge and the mihrab apse but elsewhere are used with restraint.

Iznik red and clear white glazes personify Ottoman decoration until the potteries dwindled away in the seventeenth century when a once extensive palette grew grey and muddy. The designs retained their vitality perhaps because they were still produced in the studio of Topkapısaray. The industry, revived in the eighteenth century by Nevşehirli Ibrahim Pasha, did not survive his fall.

Ceilings were painted and gilded, especially those under the galleries of mosques. Paint was also lavished on walls and domes and no dome has suffered more than that of Süleymaniye, which was once akin to that of the restored tomb of the sultan, from crude nineteenth century *trompe-l'oeil*, a technique that fascinated Osman III one hundred years before. One seventeenth century ceiling survives in all its splendour at Topkapısaray and there are others in mosques including that of Takkeci Ibrahim Çavuş outside the walls of Istanbul whose tiles are only rivalled by those of the mosque of Ramazan Efendi. Classical dome decoration also appears in miniature inside the lids of Qur'an boxes.

Stained glass was cut into small pieces and set in plaster to form arabesque and floral designs but by the eighteenth century it was used in strips and swags as the border of large, clear plates. Sinan, however, in pursuit of light employed clear glass to the limit of the load-bearing capacity of cut stone: indeed, he took the exploration of luminous space as far as it could go before modern plate glass and steel frame construction. The mosque of Mihrimah in Istanbul is the outstanding example while at that of Murat III in Manisa, built by proxy in his old age, the upper sets of lights slope inwards. At the Zal Mahmut Pasha mosque he stacked windows tier on tier until it approaches the height of a sky-scraper.

Bottle glass was inserted into the domes of *hamams* creating romantic shafts of sunshine. The baths were centres of social life, although divided by class and trade and more intimate than the public baths of Rome. The domed disrobing room has sofas, a central fountain and an alcove in which to make coffee. A low door leads into the cool room where clothes were laundered and preparation made for the hot room with its marble slab for massage under a dome, basins for washing and corner closets for privacy. Some baths were enriched with *opus sectile* work like that found on the floors of the casement recesses of major mosques.

Double Porticoes

The hamam was usually a handsome building even in the country where Sinan sometimes economized by substituting double porticoes for courtyards if there were sufficient Byzantine columns available and also where there was no room for a courtyard as with market mosques which were built over shops and a central depot. At Lüleburgaz, however, the double portico is combined with a large court-

yard to compensate for the relatively small size of the prayer hall when travellers crowded into the *kervansaray* which it served: for the Ottomans continued to build these public inns as lavishly as the Seljuks had done before them.

The mosque of Piyale Pasha near the Golden Horn exuded galleries on three sides as if turning its courtyard inside out. The minaret is set centrally on the north front where the portal should be and so more modest entrances were placed at either end of the facade. Its six large domes derive from those of the Great Mosque at Bursa and are supported by piers incorporated into the walls which require heavy buttressing and by two gigantic antique columns that rival those used in the mosques of Beyazit II and Süleyman I.

Innovating when most men are dead, Sinan's final mosques were sombrely roofed in lead which extended over drums and the large arches which support the dome. For Şemsi Ahmet Pasha he built an enchanted miniature complex with a garden onto the Bosphorus. Seaside sites pleased him as his early Mihrimah complex stretching along the nearby hillside shows. Its double portico extends to a gazebo in which the fountain is set under an ornamental bronze grille as a protection against the birds.

The Classical Finale and the Flowering of Baroque

Sinan died in 1588: his students worked on. The Yeni Valide mosque was begun by Davut Agha, the new royal architect, but was abandoned on the death of Murat III in 1603 to be completed sixty years later together with the Spice Bazaar. Yet another, more grandiose version of the Şehzade plan than that of the Valide was Mehmet Agha's for the mosque of Ahmet I which is best known for its later blue stencilling and the 21,000 tiles that broke the back of the Iznik potteries. The dome is a disappointing 23.50 metres in diameter and the stalactite plasterwork rambles over the arches. When seen from the *saray* gate the profile of domescape and six minarets is superb but when seen from the Hippodrome the composition is languid when compared with the tensed mass between four 70 metre high minarets of the Selimiye. No student possessed Sinan's vision nor could any develop the dynamic of his masterpiece.

During the seventeenth century the classical forms persisted but buildings grew smaller until in the eighteenth Ahmet III and his remarkable minister, Nevşehirli Ibrahim Pasha, introduced the Tulip Period with a plethora of pavilions in the meadows of the Sweet Waters of Europe at the head of the Golden Horn. The mob destroyed them, murdered the grand vizir and deposed the sultan. Their fountains survived. The best known stands at the palace gate but is only one of many erected during the reign.

This prelude to the Baroque Period was inspired by Yermi-sekiz Ibrahim Pasha who returned from an embassy to Paris with plans and elevations of Marley-le-Roi and Versailles, orange trees and champagne. Baroque floriates everything small like fountains – for water is baroque by nature – but nothing could overcome the convention of the domed square which all too perfectly contrasts earthly with heavenly space.

Howsoever the dome buttresses of the mosque of Nuruosmaniye cavort, the underlying form is not baroque any more than at Laleli where grand stairways ascend to the mosque. Stairs are also a feature of the Ayasma mosque at Üsküdar for both buildings seek to soar.

The unique horseshoe form of the court of Nuruosmaniye and the spectacular ramp and bridge which span the outer precinct are truly baroque. The kiosk of the Ayasma mosque is raised on pillars beside it and the cistern after which it is named. Such kiosks began with the pavilion beside the Ahmediye mosque and the palatial kiosk of the Valide mosque which was approached by a covered carriage ramp. Later these retiring rooms were placed in front of mosques as they had been long before at Bursa: an unconscious act of revivalism born of convenience. A charming innovation that spread during the eighteenth century was the carving of elaborate stone dovecotes on the walls and gates to important foundations; but the kiosks for water set at the corners of precincts long epitomised Turkish art and elegance in western eyes far more than the great masterpieces of the sixteenth century.

Flimsy materials permitted spritely cadences unthinkable in costly stone. Tall *ocaks* or fireplaces were made of plaster instead of bronze and ceilings were embellished with gilded foliage. Affection for the fragile survived the manhandling of the Beaux Arts style regurgitated by the prolific Balian family until foreign architects introduced the caprices and conceits of Art Nouveau. Such uninhibited fun was attacked by a paradoxical revivalist movement born of nationalism as hostile as possible to precisely that multiracialism that had created the former Ottoman greatness which they now sought to restore. Finally, crushed under the Teutonic ministries of an austere republic, 600 years of genius lay dead.

Architects and Materials

The architects had been trained as carpenters and engineers: the bridge at Büyükçekmice is the only work of Sinan eulogised on his tomb. He had also built pontoon bridges, barges and a system of conduits and aqueducts that brought water to the Süleymaniye complex – which had cost less than these waterworks.

Ahmet Dalgıç – The Diver or hydraulic engineer – completed his training by making a Qur'an box and before succeeding Davut Agha as its architect had driven the piers into the mud that sustain the Yeni Valide mosque. Mehmet Agha, who built Ahmet I's complex, was a musician and a worker in mother-of-pearl.

The timber of Anatolia and Rumania supplied the centering without which building in stone is impossible. Repetitive domes, moreover, meant that it could be continually reused and encouraged that standardization which is a root of Ottoman achievement. Geometry had to be simple since masons used unnotched rules and pegs and ropes for measurements.

The proportions of buildings recurred because the flow of stress predetermines architectural forms: if the width of an arch does not relate to its radius or the height of a column to its diameter, they will collapse. Once the diameter and height of a central dome was fixed structural mechanics ordained that the square beneath it should form one quarter of the total area of the ground plan. Structural limitations fertilized creativity.

Only late examples of plans have been found at Topkapısaray but early ones certainly existed in the form of simple grids and circles framed by elevations in the two-dimensional manner of the miniature. Model forts were built for mock combats and in the guild processions architects carried large flats cut out in the form of mosques. Thus a foreman could follow the lines of the foundations and check how the elevations were organized.

Materials also determine form. Limestone was plentiful and the marble quarries at Proconessus, Marmara Island, never closed but, since the art of scooping out columns had been lost and segmental examples from antiquity were rejected, Byzantine monoliths were essential for Ottoman buildings. Their stability necessitated tiebeams in the Byzantine manner: and since the dimensions of a column determines those of the arch that spans it, the scale of a portico was imposed by them.

At first buildings were roofed in tile as in Byzantine times but the Ottomans designed special tiles to fit the curvature of their domes instead of chipping them to size. Once lead became available, it was preferred: hence the title *Kurşunlu*, or Leaded, given to important provincial mosques.

Ashlar was so well cut that mortar was only used as a lubricant during erection. This also led to uniformity of form and mass – brutally so with the mosque of the Valide at Manisa – impossible to achieve with Byzantine brick. This regularity and its symbolic intransigence enabled subordinates to build justly proportioned monuments. Delegation was facilitated by the use of pendentives in place of idiosyncratic squinches or the triangulated dome supports of the early Ottoman period. Mistakes did occur. The masons at Erzerum were unable to build semi-domes and resorted to vaulting at the mosque of Lala Mustafa Pasha. They secured the stunted minaret to the corner of the building because of their experience with earthquakes.

The order of building proceeded from mosque hall to portico and minaret. Work was delegated to teams of masons which resulted in the minarets of Beyazit II's mosque at Edirne blocking the corner windows of the completed annexes.

There was an adequate flow of apprentices for so long as the levy of Christian youths into the Janissary Corps continued. The recruits were toughened by heavy work on building sites but older janissaries were lazy and given to brawling so were only called upon in an emergency. They had to work on fortresses when on campaign although numerous architects, masons and craftsmen were sent with the army. Rumeli Hisar, the finest fortress of its day, was built in three months with military precision and labour. Fortifications are supranational by the nature of warfare and in the eighteenth century were designed by foreign engineers like the Baron de Tott.

In peacetime, craftsmen were summoned when needed and the office of the Chief Architect knew where to find good workmen who were listed by name. Nomads and gypsies were conscripted for rough work and were paid wages like the craftsmen but at a much lower rate. By the end of the sixteenth century, these differential rates increased the inflationary trend of a weakening currency because private builders seduced workers from the imperial service with offers of higher wages.

Even when the days of glory were gone, unmistakably Ottoman monuments were built all over the empire. To this day, from the Balkans to Arabia there remains an Ottoman presence not solely due to the domed mosques and their slender minarets but also to the endlessly variable vernacular style of domestic architecture throughout the towns of the lost provinces. The houses are frail and doomed but their cantilevering and piers which Le Corbusier so admired before World War I fertilized western ideas in the first half of the present century. Like shadow puppets, theirs is the imagination that brings to life an age that expressed its greatness in monuments of stone.

Time Chart

Events		Ottoman Mosques	Other Monuments
1326	Orhan takes Bursa.	Haci Özbek, Iznik.	Doge's Palace.
1331	Iznik captured.	Orhan Gazi, Bilecik.	Alhambra.
1362	Murat takes Edirne.	Orhan Gazi, Bursa.	Varamin mosque.
1389	Beyazit I, sultan.	Hüdavendigâr, Bursa.	Loggia dei Lanzi.
1402	Timur defeats Beyazit.	Beyazit I, Bursa.	Seville Cathedral.
1402	Civil War.	Ulu Cami, Bursa.	Pazzi Chapel.
1413	Mehmet I prevails.	Green Complex, Bursa.	Gur Emir Tomb.
1431	Murat II, sultan.	Üç Şerefeli, Edirne.	Ducal Palace, Urbino.
1451	Mehmet II, sultan.	Fatih Complex, İst.	Palazzo Venezia.
1453	Constantinople falls	Çinili Kiosk, Ist.	Cancelleria.
1481	Beyazit II, sultan.	Beyazit II, Edirne.	Blois.
1509	Selim the Grim, sultan.	Beyazit II, Amasya.	Laurenziana.
1509	Earthquake.	Beyazit II, Istanbul.	St. Basil, Kremlin.
1516	Conquest of Syria.	Selim I, Istanbul.	St. Peter's.
1517	Conquest of Egypt.	Şehzade, Istanbul.	Villa Rotunda.
1521	Süleyman in Balkans.	Süleymaniye, Ist.	S. Giorgio Maggiore.
1529	Ist siege of Vienna.	Selimiye, Edirne.	Akbar's Tomb
1566	Selim II, sultan.	Muradiye, Manisa.	Himeji Castle, Japan.
1574	Murat III, sultan.	Yeni Valide, Ist.	Masjid-i Shah.
1603	Ahmet I, sultan.	Ahmediye, Istanbul.	Taj Mahal.
1623	Murat IV, sultan.	Baghdad Kiosk, Ist.	Place des Vosges.
1638	Baghdad captured.	Yeni Valide completed, Ist.	Versailles.
1682	2nd siege of Vienna.		Belvedere, Vienna.
1703	Ahmet III, sultan.	Hekimoğlu, Istanbul.	
1730	Popular uprising.	Ahmet III, fountain.	St. Paul's.
1754	Osman III, sultan.	Nuruosmaniye, Ist.	Schloss Brühl.
1766	Istanbul earthquake.	Laleli, Istanbul.	Radcliffe Library.
1774	Abdülhamit I, sultan.	New Fatih, Istanbul.	Baltimore Cathedral.
1807	Selim III murdered.	Beylerbey Complex.	
1808	Mahmut II, sultan.	Eyup Sultan rebuilt.	Pantheon, Paris.
1826	Janissaries slain.	Nusretye, Istanbul.	Old Museum, Berlin.
1853	Crimean War.	Dolmabahçe Place.	Houses of Parliament.
1922	Sultanate abolished.	Bebek, Istanbul.	Paris Opera House.
			Villa Savoie.

Glossary

Agha (Ağa)	Senior rank below Pasha; landowner.
Arasta	Covered market producing revenue for a mosque.
Cami	A Friday congregational mosque as opposed to a mescit.
Çavuş	Court official; sergeant-at-arms; rank below agha.
Çeşme	A tap for drinking water, often elaborate with basin.
Dervish	Member of a sect dedicated to a semi-secret path.
Hacı	A Muslim who has made the pilgrimage to Mecca.
Hamam	A public or private bath for ritual cleansing.
Han	Merchant lodgings over stores forming a court.
Hisar	Castle or fortress sometimes called a *kale*.
Imaret	A public kitchen and refectory for students, poor etc..
Kervansaray	Palace of the Caravan or inn usually in the country with stables, dormitories, lodgings, shops, smiths etc..
Konak	A mansion divided into harem for family and selamlik.
Külliye	Religious complex of college, hostel, hamam, kitchen.
Mahfil	Gallery; hence *hünkâr mahfile* or royal loge.
Medrese	A college for students of religion and religious law.
Mescit	Chapel without a minber for delivering Friday sermon.
Mihrab	Or kible. Niche indicating the direction of Mecca.
Minber	Stairs to hooded platform used as a pulpit. Important because the Friday sermon, hütbe, included edicts.
Namazgâh	Open air place of prayer sometimes having a minber.
Ocak	Tall hood-shaped chimney breast.
Sadrazam	The Grand Vizir as opposed to Vizer-azam, chief vizir.
Saray	A palace or complex of kiosks, courts and halls.
Sufi	As opposed to orthodox Sunni, followers of a secret way to Grace.
Şadirvan	The ablution fountain in a mosque court, later a tank.
Şerefe	The balcony of a minaret where muezzins call to prayer.
Tekke	Dergâh, hanikâh; convent for dervishes.
Türbe	Mausoleum or tomb deriving from Seljuk kümbets.
Ulema	The most qualified officers of law and faith under the Seyh-ül-Islam, Grand Mufti- a conservative senate.
Yalı	Mansion on the shores of the Bosphorus, with gardens.
Zaviye	A meeting house for prayer with communal rooms attached, sometimes a kitchen. Passed from Ahi to dervish use.

Bibliography

Arseven C E. *L'art turc depuis son origine jusqu'à nos jours*, Istanbul, 1939.
Aslanapa O. *Turkish art and architecture*, London, 1971.
Choiseul-Gouffier, Comte de. *Voyage pittoresque de la Grèce*, 2 vol., Paris, 1782.
Dwight H G. *Constantinople, old and new*, New York, 1913.
Egli E. *Sinan, der Baumeister osmanischer Glanzzeit*, Zurich, 1954.
Ettinghausen R. Ipsiroglu M S. Eyuboglu S. *Turkey; the ancient miniatures*, UNESCO, New York, 1961.
Eyice S. *Instanbul: petit guide à travers les monuments byzantins et turcs*, Instanbul, 1955.
Fehérvári G. *Islamic pottery, a comprehensive study on the Barlow collection*, London, 1973.
Gabriel A. *Une capitale turque, Brousse (Bursa)*, Paris, 1958.
Gabriel A. *Château turcs du Bosphore*, Paris, 1943.
Gabriel A. *Les monuments turcs d'Anatolie*, I, II, Paris, 1931–4.
Gabriel A. *Voyages archèologiques dans la Turquie Orientale*, Paris, 1940.
Goodwin G. *A history of Ottoman architecture*, London, 1971.
Grenville H. *Observations sur l'état actuel de l'Empire Ottomane*, Michigan, 1965.
Grube E J. *The World of Islam*, New York, 1967.
Gurlitt C. *Die Baukunst Konstantinopels*, 4 folios, Berlin, 1912.
Hoag J D. *Western Islamic Architecture*, New York, 1963.
Inalcik H. *The Ottoman Empire (the Classical Age 1300–1600)*, London, 1973.
Kuran A. *The Mosque in Early Ottoman Architecture*, Chicago, 1968.
Lane A. *Early Islamic Pottery*, 1947.
Lane A. *Later Islamic Pottery*, 1957.
Le Corbusier (C E Jeanneret-Gris). *My Work*, trans. Palmes, London, 1960.
Levey M. *The World of Ottoman Art*, London, 1975.

Mantran R. *Istanbul dans la seconde moitié du XII siècle*, Paris, 1962.
Mayer L A. *Islamic architects and their works*, Geneva, 1956.
Melling A I. *Voyage pittoresque de Constantinople et des rives du Bosphore*, 2 vols, Paris, 1819.
Meredith-Owens G M. *Turkish miniatures*, London, 1963.
Meyer-Riefstahl R. *Turkish architecture in Southwestern Anatolia*, Cambridge, Mass., 1931.
Otto-Dorn K. *Das Islamische Iznik*, Berlin, 1941.
Otto-Dorn K. *Die Kunst des Islams*, Baden-Baden, 1964.
Pardoe J. *The city of the Sultan, and domestic manners of the Turks in 1836*, 3 vols., London, 1838.
Penzer N M. *The Harem*, London, 1936.
Sherrard P. *Constantinople*, Oxford, 1965.
Sumner-Boyd H. *Strolling through Istanbul*, Istanbul, 1972.
Talbot Rice D. *Islamic Art*, Harmondsworth, 1965.
Unsal B. *Turkish Islamic architecture in Seljuk and Ottoman times*, London, 1959.
Vogt-Göknil U. *Les mosquées turques*, Zurich, 1953.
Vogt-Göknil U. *Turquie ottomane*, Fribourg, 1965.
Wittik P. *The rise of the Ottoman Empire*, London, 1938.

Important articles on aspects of Ottoman architecture appear in the volumes of the 1st and 2nd congress of Turkish Art, published in Ankara and Naples, respectively, and in the following journals: *AARP*, 9, London; *Ars Islamica*, I, III, IV, V, XV–XVI, Michigan; *Ars Orientalis*, II, Michigan; and *Art Bulletin*, XII,4 and XLV,3. The principal work of reference is the *Dictionary of Islam*. Works in the Turkish language have not been listed; the most important Turkish journals which contain papers on Ottoman buildings are the *Vakiflar Dergisi* and *Belletin*.

Index

Plate 1 Orhan Gazi Mosque, Bilecik, early 14th century. This mosque has a dome 16.50 metres high and some 10 metres wide carried on primitive squinches between deep arches which form the shallow arms of a cross. Beyond the truncated minaret is a dervish retreat. The twin minarets are a nineteenth century attempt to relight the lamp of Ottoman glory. (Photo: G. Goodwin)

Plate 2 Yıldırım Complex, Mausoleum of Beyazit 1. This is a typical Ottoman royal tomb complete with a handsome porch. Here Murat IV came to insult his unlucky ancestor who after a life of victories depending on the mobility of his forces was captured by Timur in 1402 and died of chagrin. (Photo: G. Goodwin)

Plate 3 Eski Cami, Edirne, minber detail. The noon sermon, including imperial edicts, was read from minbers originally reserved for major mosques. The design of the carved flanks was based on interlacing hexagons or octagons within the frame of a wheel set in an equilateral triangle. (Photo: W. Ball)

35

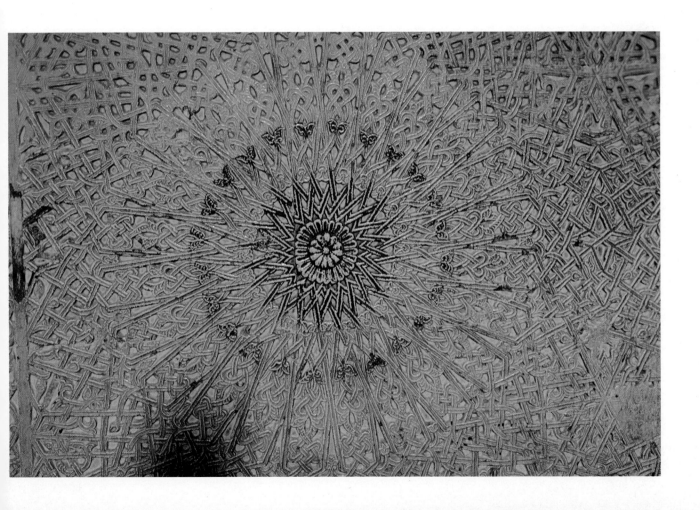

Plate 4 Üç Şerefeli Cami (Mosque of the Three Balconies), Edirne, begun 1437. Named from the balconies of the tallest of its four minarets, which vary in style and date, it was the Great Mosque until Sinan built that of Süleymaniye. The massive piers divide the interior spaces. (Photo: W. Ball)

Plate 5 Beyazit II Complex, Edirne, hospital hall, 1484. The great hall of the hospital with bays and corner rooms set about a spacious pool is crowned by a dome. It is worth noting the extravagant thickening of the triangular corners resulting from the hexagonal plan, typical of the Ottoman search for a considerable margin of safety. (Photo: W. Ball)

Plate 6 Mevlana Tekke (Convent), Konya, 13th to 18th centuries. The original
Seljuk buildings have been rebuilt or altered and the appearance of all except the
tomb of the great mystical poet, Rumi, with its modern reproduction tiles, belongs to
the reigns of Süleyman I and Selim II in the main. (Photo: A. Hutt)

Plate 7 Haseki Hürrem Complex, Istanbul, 1539. Architect: Sinan. The work
may have been started by his predecessor as royal architect, Acemi Ali. It included a
hospital for women, a soup kitchen for the poor and a medical school. It was built for
for the wife of Süleyman I, known in the west as Roxelane. (Photo: J. Raby)

Plate 8 Süleymaniye Complex, Istanbul, 1557, passage between colleges. This alley leads between the two upper colleges to the piazza that stretches before the mosque precinct. On the left and right are two stone residences for the directors which are the only houses still standing that can be attributed to Sinan and they still make agreeable residences. (Photo: J. Raby)

Plate 9 Süleymaniye, Istanbul, view over roofs of lower colleges. On the Horn side of the complex, the two colleges are not raised on the platform but descend the hillside in a series of steps so as to avoid masking the mosque and mausoleum of the sultan. The lowest rank of cells rides over those of the preparatory college. (Photo: J. Raby)

Plate 10 Rüstem Pasha Mosque, Istanbul, 1561. Architect: Sinan. The great and unloved Grand Vizir did not live to see the mosque completed with its outstanding collection of Iznik tiles, some of the best of which were reserved for his tomb. The mosque is set above the bustle of the bazaar over a depot and small shops. (Photo: W. Ball)

Plate 11 Rüstem Pasha Mosque, Istanbul, tile. Of all Iznik motifs the tulip is the most famous. These tiles cover a supporting pier, for the mosque plan is an octagon inscribed in a rectangle, and are examples of the pure white ground on which the prevailing red and blue design is depicted. (Photo: J. Raby)

Plate 12 Rüstem Pasha Mosque, Istanbul, tile. This detail from an exterior panel is an example of the vitality of the designs which were drawn by the artists of the palace studio and sent to the potters at Iznik for transfer to the tile panels and plates that were exported all over Europe. (Photo: J. Raby)

Plate 13 Tekke (Convent), Damascus, mid-16th century. Architect: Sinan, by proxy. The foundation of Süleyman I was a kitchen for pilgrims to Mecca with a great court and pool before the mosque, shaded by trees in the Syrian manner. The tiles were also locally made. (Photo: G. Goodwin)

Plate 14 Piyale Pasha Mosque, Istanbul, 1573. The placing of the minaret in the centre of the facade is unusual although not unique. The large domes are supported by buttresses incorporated in the thickness of the walls and by two immense free-standing columns. (Photo: G. Goodwin)

Plate 15 Selimiye Complex, Edirne, 1569–75. Architect: Sinan. The mosque was built on top of the hill overlooking the town when Sinan was nearly 80. The dome is the largest in Ottoman history and is massed between the four loftiest minarets and so the lesser buildings of the complex are dwarfed. (Photo: W. Ball)

Plate 16 Selimiye Complex, Edirne, mosque courtyard. Sinan did not repeat the grand entry of Süleymaniye but returned to an older tradition of even height of domes. The arcades are remarkably broad as are the portico domes, achieving an effect of great space beautifully articulated as with the lesser vaults beside the cupola before the great door. (Photo: J. Raby)

Plate 17 Selimiye Complex, Edirne, mosque interior. Selim II, son of Süleyman the Magnificent and Haseki Hürrem or Roxelane, daughter of a Greek priest, was obese and notorious for his love of wine. But he was not a sot and his poetry has a permanent place in Ottoman literature. (Photo: W. Ball)

Plate 18 Selimiye Complex, Edirne, mosque interior. Sinan was determined to achieve perfection and the quality of the tiles, carving of the minber and fluting of the piers add to the splendour of the ordered immensity of this interior. The eight piers achieve a circular movement which pivots on the central singing gallery. (Photo: W. Ball)

Plate 19 Selimiye Complex, Edirne, ceiling. This design is an example of the Islamic passion for relating areas and objects of disparate size and purpose through their decoration. This pattern could be applied to a book or rug just as well as to a ceiling. Although repainted, the work is likely to be modelled on the original. (Photo: J. Raby)

Plate 20 Muradiye Complex, Manisa, 1583–86. Architect: Sinan, by proxy, but he may have visited the site on his return from the Pilgrimage. His first deputy, Mahmut, died and was succeeded by Mehmet Agha, who built the complex of Ahmet I in Istanbul. Manisa was a favourite retreat of Ottoman sultans. (Photo: G. Goodwin)

Plate 21 Ivaz Efendi Mosque, Istanbul, about 1581–5.
Architect: probably a student of Sinan. Iznik tiles imitate marblework with varying degrees of success. Here ceramic replaces the usual revolving colonettes each side of the mihrab. The tiles in this mosque are of outstanding quality. (Photo: J. Raby)

Plate 22 Zal Mahmut Pasha Complex, Istanbul, 1580, mausoleum. Architect: Sinan. The brutish pasha strangled the struggling Prince Mustafa in his tent at Amasya when Süleyman I condemned his son for treason. Mahmut Pasha was rewarded in his old age by marriage to a royal widow. (Photo: G. Goodwin)

Plate 23 **Yeni Valide Complex, Istanbul, begun 1597–1603, completed 1663.** Architects: Davut Agha and Dalgiç Ahmet Agha for Safiye, Queen Mother of Mehmet III. An equally formidable dowager, Turhan Hadice Sultan employed Mustafa the Patcher-up to complete the work. He had repaired the fortresses along the Bosphorus. (Photo: G. Goodwin)

**Plate 24 Baghdad Kiosk,
Topkapısaray, Istanbul, 1638.**
Architect: Hasan Agha although
Koca Kasim Agha was royal
architect at the time. The grand
room with its reused tiles, gilded
woodwork, inlaid shutters and doors,
and a great bronze hood to the
fireplace was built by Murad IV to
celebrate the reconquest of Baghdad
shortly before his powerful
personality and physique were
destroyed by debauchery.
(Photo: J. Raby)

Plate 1 Haci Özbek Mosque, Iznik, 1333. The first known Ottoman mosque which can be dated by an inscription. Earlier examples existed and some have been rebuilt. The original plan was regular and a mature work with an 8 metre wide dome carried on triangular supports. The portico was demolished. (Photo: G. Goodwin)

Plate 2 Orhan Gazi Mosque, Bursa, begun 1339. This heavily restored royal chapel of Orhan, the Warrior for the Faith, has zaviye or hostel rooms for dervishes. The deep five-bay porch in the early Ottoman style admits to the vestibule of the central inner court. (Photo: G. Goodwin)

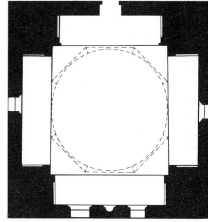

Fig. 1 Mosque of Orhan Gazi, Bilecik

Plate 3 Süleyman Pasha College, Iznik, early 14th century. This medrese or college of law and theology was built by the brother of Orhan I, the first pasha and a great soldier, in place of a converted monastery. The plan is typical of later colleges with study halls, cells and porticoes on three sides of a court. (Photo: Michael Stewart Thompson)

Plate 4 Hüdavendigâr Mosque, Çekirge, near Bursa, 1365–85. Hüdavendigâr means royal and reflects the imperial longings of Murat I. There are Seljuk examples of two-storey colleges but the erection of an orthodox college above a retreat for heterodox dervishes is extraordinary. (Photo: G. Goodwin)

Plate 5 Hüdavendigâr Complex, Çekirge, Batchelors' Hamam.
This modest wash-house for the students at the college of Murat I is still in use. Its humble proportions and sturdy workmanship belong to the earlier days of the Ottoman dynasty before conquests had brought trade as well as booty. (Photo: G. Goodwin)

Plate 6 Nilufer Hatun Zaviye, Iznik, 1338. The zaviye is large and well-restored including notable plasterwork in the domes. It was built by Murat I in honour of his mother, daughter of a Christian baron, who was a woman of strong personality and who was regent when Orhan was away on campaign. (Photo: G. Goodwin)

Plate 7 Isa Bey Mosque, Ayasluğ (Seljuk Ephesus), 1374. The mosque was built by a rival of the Ottomans, the bey or lord of Aydin. Although the domes and aisle roofs have collapsed it is still a monumental example of the Damascus style. It is not known what was the exact form of the courtyard arcades. (Photo: Turkish Ministry of Tourism)

Plate 8 Isa Bey Mosque, facade. The facade windows are richly carved in the Syrian manner using marble from the ruins of the great city close at hand. The minarets are awkwardly perched above the side entrances to the court, yet the portals contrive to be exceptionally monumental. (Photo: G. Goodwin)

Plate 9 Yıldırım Beyazit Complex, Bursa, 1390–5. The large complex was built by Beyazit the Thunderbolt whose emblem is incorporated into the decoration either in lead or tile. The court under a dome 22 metres high by 12 metres wide is divided from the prayer hall by a hipped 'Bursa' arch. (Photo: R. R. E. Chorley)

Plate 10 Yıldırım Beyazit Complex, college courtyard. This long and narrow medrese was heavily restored and glazed and this detracts from the three-dimensional power of the original open arcades. The ruined hospital was similar in plan and both were decorated with celestial symbols. (Photo: G. Goodwin)

Plate 11 Yıldırım Beyazit Complex, college exterior. An open market was probably held beside the college from its inception. The typical use of alternating layers of brick and stone, although decorative, was a measure of economy long practised by Byzantine builders. (Photo: G. Goodwin)

Plate 12 Firuz Agha Mosque, Milas, 1394. This is a small provincial building erected by the Ottoman governor, but with a grand portico and rich carving. The minaret is set at the corner of the prayer hall beyond the inner court which was the logical position with Bursa style mosques. (Photo: G. Goodwin)

Plate 13 Firuz Agha Mosque, Milas. The thick and deepset portico was a feature of Bursa type mosques which in the provinces achieved a sense of power and grandeur which is here matched by the forcefulness of the design of chevrons incorporated into the arches. (Photo: G. Goodwin)

Plate 14 Great Mosque (Ulu Cami), Bursa, 1396–9. The first large congregational mosque of the Ottomans measures 56 by 68 metres over all. The twenty domes rest on pendentives – not Turkish triangles – and twelve cruciform piers are decorated with giant inscriptions probably based on the original script. (Photo: Turkish Ministry of Tourism)

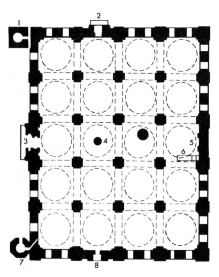

Fig. 2 Great Mosque, Bursa

1 Northeast minaret
2 Northeast entry
3 Great North Door
4 Pool
5 Mihrab
6 Minber
7 Northwest minaret
8 Northwest entry

Plate 15 Old Mosque (Eski Cami), Edirne, 1402–13. Architect: Hacı Ala'ettin of Konya, builder: Ömer ibn Ibrahim. Begun by Prince Süleyman, completed by his victorious rival, Mehmet, the mosque has suffered from fire and earthquake. Porch and minaret are additions. The prayer hall is 50 metres square. (Photo: W. Ball)

Plate 16 Beyazit Pasha Mosque, Amasya, 1414–19. Architect: Yakup ibn
Aptullah. The loyal vizir of Mehmet I united his mosque and large dervish hostel
behind a stalwart facade. There was no fountain because the river which runs
alongside was used instead. (Photo: G. Goodwin)

Plate 17 Green Mosque (Yeşil Cami) and Complex, Bursa, 1412–19.
Architect: the Vizir Hacı Ivaz Pasha, decorator: Ali ibn Ilyas Ali. The sultan died
before a portico was built in front of the richly carved facade with its open loggias.
(Photo: G. Goodwin)

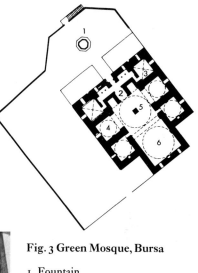

Fig. 3 Green Mosque, Bursa

1 Fountain
2 Vestibule
3 Hostel room
4 Alcove
5 Interior court
6 Prayer hall

73

Plate 18 Green Complex, Bursa, mausoleum of Mehmet I. Hacı Ivaz completed the tomb after his master's death with a dome 15 metres in diameter which dominates those of the mosque below. The splendid mihrab, like that of the mosque, matches richness with elan. (Photo: G. Goodwin)

Plate 19 Murat II Mosque, Edirne, 1421. There was a monastery or tekke of the Mevlevi dervishes attached to the mosque which was damaged in the earthquake of 1751. The interior has vestiges of paintwork, a fine mihrab, and notable tiles in a Chinese style. It is a suburban foundation. (Photo: G. Goodwin)

Plate 20 Üç Şerefeli Mosque, Edirne, courtyard. The width of the courtyard was determined by the two wings with their separate entrances deriving from the Bursa zaviye rooms. The arches of the arcades could only join the loftier portico by splitting their capitals, a problem unresolved at Süleymaniye. (Photo: W. Ball)

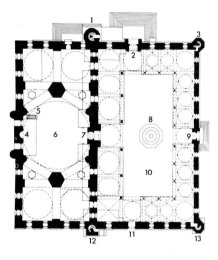

Fig. 4 Mosque of Üç Şerefeli, Edirne

1, 3, 12 and 13 Minarets
2, 9 and 11 Entrances
4 Mihrab
5 Minber
6 Prayer Hall
7 Great entry to mosque
8 Fountain
10 Courtyard

Plate 21 Rumeli Hisar (Castle), Istanbul, 1452. The Cut-Throat, New or Good Castle was built in four months due to careful planning. A vizir was responsible for each tower and the sultan, Mehmet II the Conqueror, for the curtain walls. At sea level there are a barbican and sally ports. (Photo: G. Goodwin)

Plate 22 Fatih Complex, Istanbul, 1463–70. Architect: Sinan. The mosque was rebuilt after the earthquake of 1766 but some of the complex survived including the eight colleges beside an esplanade carried on vaults, about 325 metres square. Such esplanades were typical of Islam and Byzantium. (Photo: Turkish Ministry of Tourism)

Plate 23 Çinili Kiosk (Tiled Pavilion), Istanbul, 1475. The Timurid plan, Sufi
inscriptions to Ali and use of brick imply that a Persian architect was at work. The
original wooden portico was burnt and rebuilt in stone in the 18th century. The plan
of the kiosk underlies almost all major domestic Ottoman buildings. (Photo:
G. Goodwin)

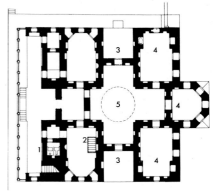

Fig. 5 Çinili Kiosk, Istanbul

1 Portico
2 Trapdoor to lower floors
3 Loggias
4 Royal apartments
5 Great hall

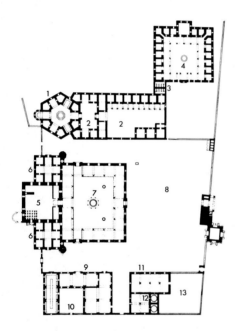

Fig. 6 Beyazit II Complex, Edirne

1 Hospital hall
2 Hospital and asylum courts
3 Latrines
4 Medical College
5 Mosque hall
6 Hostel
7 Mosque court
8 Precinct
9 Great kitchen
10 Kitchen yard
11 Store
12 Bakehouse
13 Service yard

Plate 24 Ishak Pasha Complex, Inegöl, about 1480. This soldier who was the chief vizir of Mehmet II was dismissed by Beyazit II and exiled to his native town. The setting is rurally spacious but the mosque is small and only the vaulted bays or iwans remain of the Bursa zaviye plan. (Photo: G. Goodwin)

Plate 25 Beyazit II Complex, Edirne, begun 1484. Architect: Hayrettin(?). This magnificent complex was devoted to the care of the sick and laid out with fine detailing. The hospital had a section for the insane and there were a medical college, kitchens, bakeries and stores beside the hostel wings each side of the mosque. (Photo: G. Goodwin)

Plate 26 Beyazit II Complex, Edirne, asylum colonnade. The cells of the asylum opened onto a fine colonnade and an extensive lawn across which were auxiliary hospital buildings and gates into the large precinct. This is a typical reuse of Byzantine marble monolithic columns essential to Ottoman building. (Photo: W. Ball)

Plate 27 Firuz Agha Mosque, Istanbul, 1491. The mosque was built above the Hippodrome by the Lord Treasurer to Beyazit II and is a perfect example of a small foundation, endowed by a minister, with its triple-domed portico, although the minaret is on the northeast corner where the houses were instead of the northwest which had become the usual position. (Photo: W. Ball)

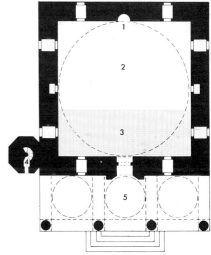

Fig. 7 Firuz Bey Mosque, Istanbul

1 Mihrab
2 Prayer hall
3 Area under gallery
4 Minaret
5 Portico

Plate 28 Beyazit II Complex, Istanbul 1501–6. Architect in Chief may have been Yakup Şah bin Sultan Şah with whom Hayrettin possibly collaborated. The hostel wings, now part of the prayer area, may have been separate units. The 17.50 metre wide dome is relatively small. The area round the mosque has been mutilated. (Photo: Turkish Ministry of Tourism)

Plate 29 Beyazit II Complex, Istanbul, mosque vestibule. The hostel wings are now open onto the prayer hall and may even have taken this form originally although this is highly unlikely. The result today is of a particularly sturdy vista through broad archways which is as exceptional as it was unintended. (Photo: W. Ball)

Plate 30 Beyazit II Complex, Istanbul, interior. The minber is seen from under the royal loge which is carried as usual on colonettes of particularly rich marbles. The capitals are stalactite in form and represent one of the two Ottoman types. The other chevron style was used in less august corners. (Photo: W. Ball)

Plate 31 Beyazit II Complex, Istanbul, grillework of minber. Underlying the designs of Ottoman architecture were forms and styles based on the old established Islamic tradition and this is an example of the interlacing fretwork which could be found all over Muslim territory. (Photo: W. Ball)

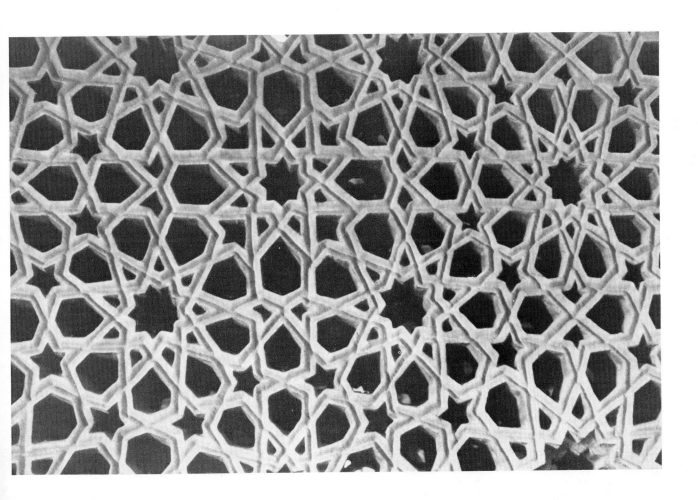

Plate 32 Battal Seyit Gazi, near Eskişehir, rebuilt 1511–17. The complex is on the top of a hill on the site of a convent. The church was converted by the Bektashi order of dervishes and greatly enlarged. Battal Gazi was a semi-mythical hero who may have married a Byzantine princess. (Photo: G. Goodwin)

Plate 33 Battal Seyit Gazi, kitchen. These ocaks or hooded fireplaces for boiling cauldrons or roasting sheep in are but part of the battery needed to feed the dervishes and the many pilgrims. There is also an extensive cellarage and lecture and recreational halls of stately dimensions. (Photo: Michael Stewart Thompson)

Plate 34 Selim I Complex, Istanbul, 1522. Architect: probably Acemi Ali and certainly not Sinan to whom much has been attributed indiscriminately. The complex reflects the form of Beyazit II's at Edirne. The courtyard is overwhelmed by the canopy over the fountain added by Murat IV. (Photo: G. Goodwin)

Plate 35 Valide (Queen Dowager) Complex, Manisa, 1522. The mosque built by Süleyman the Magnificent in honour of his mother Hafise Hatun, has an uncompromising pre-Sinan Ottoman silhouette exactly expressing its structure. The complex was first restored with baroque zest and again more soberly recently. (Photo: Turkish Ministry of Tourism)

Plate 36 Valide Complex, Manisa, hamam. The bath has been rebuilt but is nonetheless an excellent example of the traditional Ottoman hamam with handsomely domed disrobing rooms and the hot chamber under a second large cupola studded with bottle glass in order to admit light. The complex includes a college round the spacious court, asylum and boys' school. (Photo: G. Goodwin)

Plate 37 Cezeri Kasim Pasha Mosque, Bozüyük, completed 1528. A typical vizirial provincial mosque but with interesting tiles and fine woodwork of which these shutters are an example. The lower casements were unglazed but protected by iron grilles. Shutters, therefore, were an essential protection against extremes of climate. (Photo: Michael Stewart Thompson)

Plate 38 Selimiye Mosque, Konya, first half of 16th century, misattributed to Sinan. The mosque, probably built by Süleyman I in honour of his conquering father, Selim I, is also a model of the original mosque of Fatih Mehmet in Istanbul but with no courtyard. The portico, however, is fine. Selim II increased the endowment. (Photo: G. Goodwin)

Fig. 8 Selimiye Mosque, Konya

1 Mihrab
2 Prayer hall
3 and 4 Minarets
5 Portico

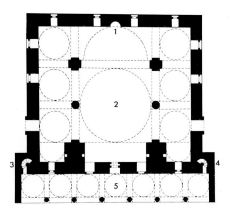

Plate 39 Selimiye Mosque, Konya, interior. The mosque contains good, late paintwork, a fine mihrab and a minber with a hood which is copied from the Seljuk-style turret over the tomb of the great mystic, Rumi, close at hand. (Photo: Michael Stewart Thompson)

**Plate 40 Mihrimah Sultan
Complex, Üsküdar, 1547–8.**
Architect: Sinan. Also called the
Iskele or Landing-Stage Mosque.
The complex lies along the hillside.
It is likely that Mihrimah's father,
Süleyman, built the complex in her
honour since only a reigning
monarch might adorn his mosque
with more than one minaret.
(Photo: G. Goodwin)

Plate 41 **Şehzade Mehmet Complex, Istanbul, mausoleum.** Architect: Sinan. Süleyman's dearly loved heir died of smallpox, full of promise at the age of 22. Sinan was never to use so ornate a style again nor to centralise a mosque so rigidly. The graveyard is remarkable for a number of fine türbes including that of Rüstem Pasha. (Photo: W. Ball)

Plate 42 Şehzade Mehmet Complex, Istanbul, 1544–8. This is the first sure handling of the turrets as anchors for the piers carrying the main dome and is a remarkable organisation of a domescape and of the logical response of the open court to the closed prayer hall; a too perfect logic led to monotony. (Photo: G. Goodwin)

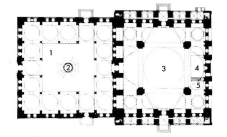

Fig. 9 Şehzade Mehmet Mosque, Istanbul

1 Court
2 Fountain
3 Prayer hall
4 Mihrab
5 Minber

Plate 43 & 44 Şehzade Mehmet Complex, Istanbul, mosque courtyard. The hood over the cistern, like many elsewhere, was added 100 years later by Murat IV. It results in a reduced sense of space and masks the grandeur of the great door. The portico also suffers to some extent. (Photo: W. Ball)

Caption on previous page

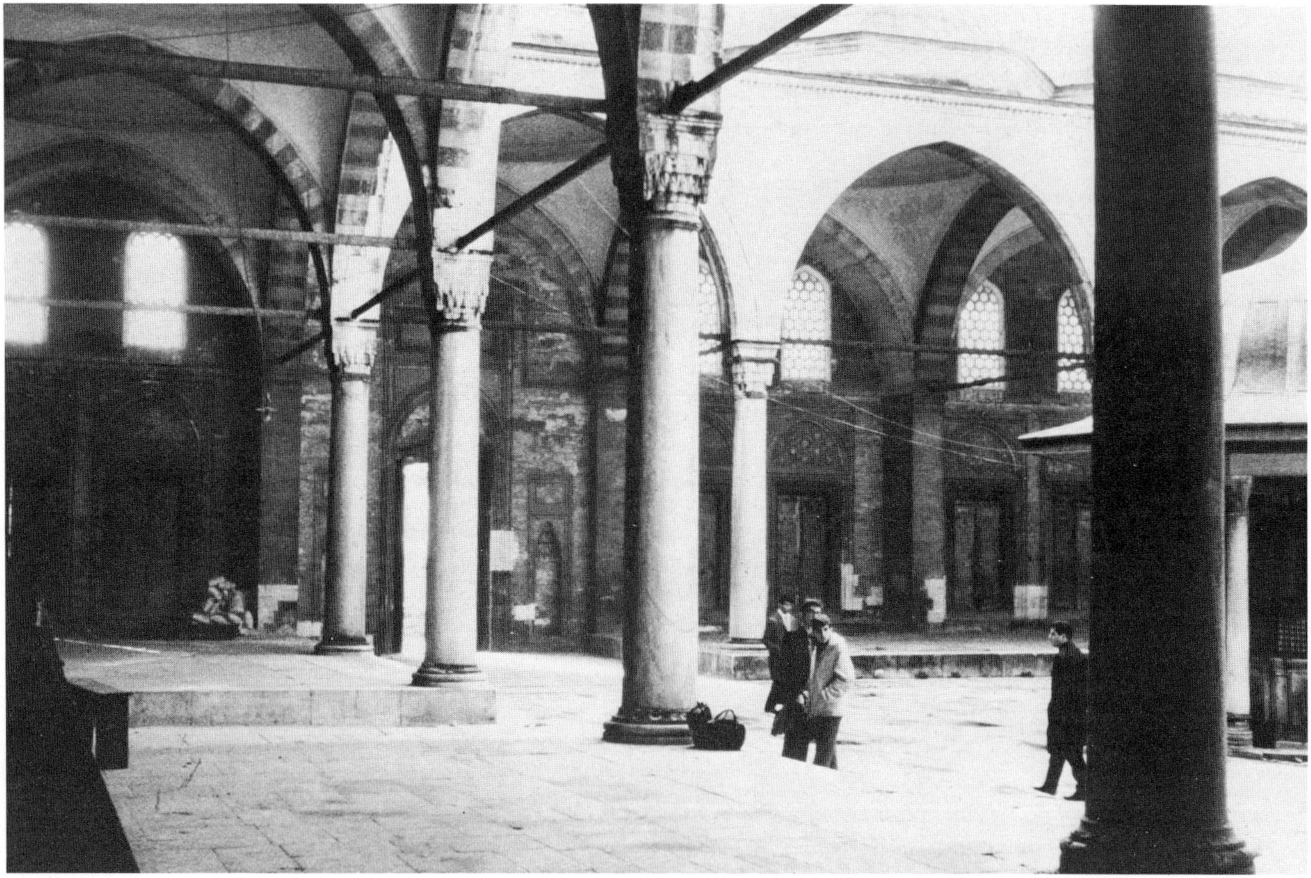

Plate 45 Şehzade Mehmet Complex, Istanbul, domes and semi-domes.
The roofs interlock like pumpkins on a market stall. It can be seen here how when a
window was inset, the wall was correspondingly thickened as if the masonry which
had been displaced by glass had to be added for safety's sake: which was true in terms
of engineering. (Photo: W. Ball)

Plate 46 Şehzade Mehmet Complex, Istanbul, inlaid soffit. Interlacing circles inset with stars form a design of considerable power which evolved in the early days of Islam. This continuity of forms is a striking aspect of Islamic decoration and at once significant of its virility and of its inability to liberate its creative impulses under a rigid religious social system. (Photo: W. Ball)

Plate 47 Şehzade Mehmet Complex, Istanbul, grille of soffit to window.
This carved stone grille forms a typical pattern used in Ottoman architecture as in all
Islamic buildings with antecedents relating to Byzantine forebears. The power of the
composition lies in a simplicity which conceals the elaboration of the interlacing.
(Photo: W. Ball)

**Plate 48 Hadım (Eunuch)
Ibrahim Pasha Mosque,
Istanbul, 1551.** Architect: Sinan.
The mosque reflects the influence of
the church of Ss. Sergius and
Bacchus on Sinan with its octagonal
form within the square. The portico
lunettes are among the earliest
embellished with Iznik tiles.
Ibrahim Pasha was Grand Vizer
under Süleyman the Magnificent.
(Photo: Artomonov Collection,
Freer Gallery of Art)

Plate 49 Süleymaniye Complex, Istanbul, 1556. Architect: Sinan. The mosque dome is 53 metres high by 26.60 metres in diameter, or exactly half the height, a proportion that Sinan was to reject. The outer minarets are shorter than those flanking the mosque itself and create a pyramidal effect in conjunction with the dome. (Photo: Turkish Ministry of Tourism)

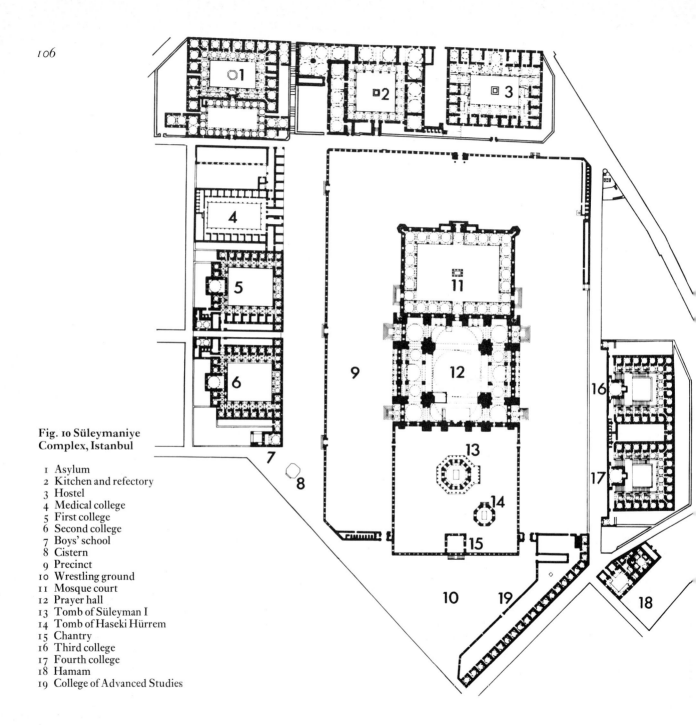

Fig. 10 Süleymaniye Complex, Istanbul

1 Asylum
2 Kitchen and refectory
3 Hostel
4 Medical college
5 First college
6 Second college
7 Boys' school
8 Cistern
9 Precinct
10 Wrestling ground
11 Mosque court
12 Prayer hall
13 Tomb of Süleyman I
14 Tomb of Haseki Hürrem
15 Chantry
16 Third college
17 Fourth college
18 Hamam
19 College of Advanced Studies

Plate 50 Süleymaniye Complex, Istanbul, mosque interior. The mihrab area was enriched with glass and tiles including the great calligraphic roundels designed by Karahisarı, the finest calligrapher at the court of the magnificent monarch. The large piers have spigots inserted for the refreshment of the faithful. (Photo: W. Ball)

Plate 51 Süleymaniye Complex, Istanbul, glass. Ottoman stained glass was imported from Venice, cut into small pieces and inserted in plaster to form floral designs. It is best viewed at an angle of 45 degrees. The glass of Süleymaniye was designed by Ibrahim Sarhoş, or the Drunkard, whose skill condoned his vices. (Photo: W. Ball)

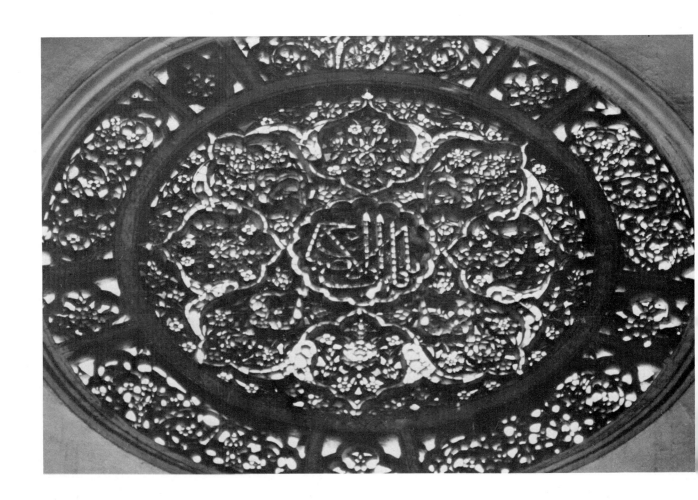

Plate 52 Süleymaniye Complex, Istanbul, plasterwork. The plasterwork, which is typical of fine Ottoman craftsmanship in the 16th century, was picked out in colour during the mid-century restoration. Here filigree bosses replace the stalactites which were sometimes moulded round a metal core. (Photo: W. Ball)

Plate 53 Süleymaniye, Istanbul, gate to precinct. The gate, with its lodging for a mosque officer above it, is an example of the elegance of the details of the complex as are the grilled windows in the wall. Indeed, small buildings such as this epitomise the Ottoman ideal. (Photo: G. Goodwin)

Plate 54 Haseki Hürrem or Aya Sofya Hamam, Istanbul, 1556. Architect: Sinan. Süleyman I built this double bath in honour of Roxelane. It is finely appointed and unusual because the men's section backs onto the women's section. The result is a landmark between the saray and the mosque of Ahmet I because of the clearance of the houses. (Photo: W. Ball)

Plate 55 Osmaniye College, Aleppo, 16th century. There are 42 cells for students and a large courtyard. The minaret is the tallest in Aleppo and a symbol of the Ottoman presence in Syria. A condition of the foundation document is that stray cats should be fed at the gate and this is still the custom. (Photo: G. Goodwin)

Plate 56 Rüstem Pasha Mosque, Istanbul. The interior is clad with tiles on every pier and wall including those at gallery level, but the 19th century paintwork is unfortunate. Later, Sinan was to employ tiles with greater discretion and finer effect on the principle that less is more. (Photo: Turkish Ministry of Tourism)

Plate 57 Rüstem Pasha Mosque, Istanbul, double portico. The courtyard area was restricted because the mosque is built over shops so the ablution fountain is at street level. Either side of the mosque door are enormous casements used also at the mosque of Kara Ahmet Pasha. Tiles proliferate over the outside walls as well as inside. (Photo: W. Ball)

Plate 58 Lala Mustafa Pasha Mosque, Ilgin, mid-16th century. The mosque is a typical vizirial mosque of provincial workmanship which did not originate from the office of the Chief Architect, Sinan, who did, however, design the adjacent kervansaray for the minister. The court is treated as a free open space without form. (Photo: G. Goodwin)

**Plate 59 Lala Mustafa Pasha
Mosque, Erzerum, 1563.**
Architect: Sinan. The royal
architect could not travel all over the
empire and work was delegated to
subordinates who depended on local
workmen. Thus this mosque has
barrel vaults for semi-domes and a
short thick minaret inset into its
corner because of the fear of
earthquakes. (Photo: Turkish
Ministry of Tourism)

Plate 60 Mihrimah Sultan Complex, Istanbul, about 1565. Architect: Sinan. This is the princess's own foundation built when she was the richest woman in the world and 'Queen Mother' to her brother, Selim II. Hence the single minaret so elegant that it collapsed during the earthquake of 1894 after which the building was repainted and reglazed. (Photo: W. Ball)

Plate 61 Mihrimah Sultan Complex, Istanbul, interior. Locally made bottle glass enabled Sinan to set tiers of windows one above the other and reduce the stonework to the minimum necessary to support the curtain wall since most of the load was borne by the corner piers and buttresses. (Photo: W. Ball)

Plate 62 Aqueducts, Belgrade Forest, Istanbul-Mağlova (Justinian's). 1567.
Architect: Sinan. The Byzantine aqueducts were in ruins when Sinan rebuilt the
system in conjunction with the great conduits bringing water from the northern hills
into the city. The longest aqueduct, the Üzünkemer, is 716 metres in length.
(Photo: Artomonov Collection, Freer Gallery of Art)

Plate 63 Semiz (Plump) Ali Pasha, Babaeski, about 1565. Architect: Sinan by proxy. The mosque stands on a height above the bridge and presents a massed exterior although some of the problems of design are unresolved which is even more true of the interior where the windows are not satisfactorily placed. (Photo: G. Goodwin)

**Plate 64 Hüsrev Pasha Mosque, Old Van, 1567 ; ruined by earthquake April
1921.** This mosque and its sister, Kaya Çelebi, are typical garrison mosques down to
the standard mihrab like that of the Great Mosque at Adılcevaz. Although erected by
rule of thumb, there are local influences including the striking horizontal striping in
the Syrian manner. (Photo: G. Goodwin)

Plate 65 Great Mosque (Ulu Cami), Adılcevaz, late 16th century. This mosque was built as a replacement for the Seljuk mosque on the hillside above Lake Van. It is a reversion to the multi-domed plan but all nine cupolas have fallen. The trefoil mihrab design is common throughout the region. (Photo: G. Goodwin)

Plate 66 Selim II Complex, Karapinar, 1569. Architect: Sinan, by proxy. Only the plan of the mosque can be attributed to Sinan and that is remarkably trim but the proportions are good and make it appear larger than it is. The complex includes a hamam which has now been restored unlike the market and the fine gateways. (Photo: Michael Stewart Thompson)

Plate 67 Piyale Pasha Mosque, Istanbul, 1573. The Grand Admiral was the son of a Croation shoemaker. His mosque is remarkable for its six large domes and its multiplicity of arcades, porticoes and galleries which were damaged in the earthquake of 1894. It is not likely to be the work of Sinan. (Photo: Artomonov Collection, Freer Gallery of Art)

Plate 68 Selimiye Complex, Edirne, mosque turrets. The eight anchor turrets are conventional in form. Already they are clad in lead the use of which Sinan found more and more appealing the older he became. Buttresses remain a feature of his work and here lead to an asymmetry which is not altogether satisfactory. (Photo: W. Ball)

Fig. 11 Selimiye Mosque, Edirne

1 Mihrab
2 Minarets
3 Prayer hall
4 Court

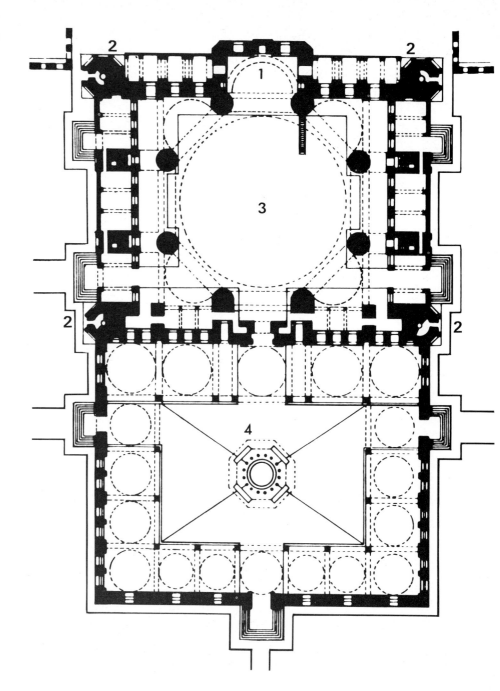

Plate 69 Selimiye Complex, Edirne, mosque domes. Sinan at this time introduced elegant onion-shaped additional turrets just as he later resorted to a Jacobean form at mosques such as that of Zal Mahmut Pasha, Istanbul. The onion shape was also used to cap his outdoor minber/dwarf minaret at Büyükçekmice. (Photo: W. Ball)

Plate 70 Selimiye Complex, Edirne, mosque courtyard. The fountain has no hood so that the full flow of space is uninterrupted. The exterior height of the portico enforces the halving of capitals where they join the colonnades. A new form of capital was introduced on the left curiously akin to some found in the Alhambra. (Photo: J. Raby)

Plate 71 Selimiye Complex, Edirne, mosque interior. Sinan's remarkable achievement architecturally was to remove the semi-domes but retain the exedras or smaller supporting domes. By extending the galleries over the outside porticoes he obviated the monotony of total centralisation. (Photo: W. Ball)

Plate 72 Selimiye Complex, Edirne, mosque interior. The floral decoration belongs to the last century but the elegant grillework with the protective bottle-glass windows behind are original. Their design belongs to a tradition dating from the earliest days of Islam. (Photo: W. Ball)

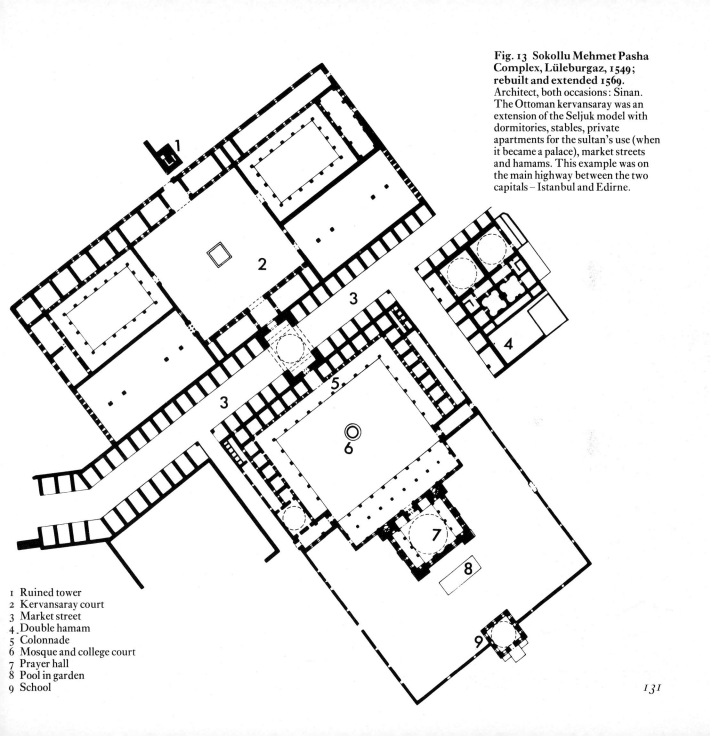

Fig. 13 Sokollu Mehmet Pasha Complex, Lüleburgaz, 1549; rebuilt and extended 1569. Architect, both occasions: Sinan. The Ottoman kervansaray was an extension of the Seljuk model with dormitories, stables, private apartments for the sultan's use (when it became a palace), market streets and hamams. This example was on the main highway between the two capitals – Istanbul and Edirne.

1 Ruined tower
2 Kervansaray court
3 Market street
4 Double hamam
5 Colonnade
6 Mosque and college court
7 Prayer hall
8 Pool in garden
9 School

Fig. 12 Sokollu Mehmet Pasha Mosque, Istanbul

Plate 73 Sokollu Mehmet Pasha Mosque, Istanbul, 1571. Architect: Sinan.
The fame of the tiles in this mosque distracts from the fine ordering of college cells
and lecture hall over the entry stairs and the lofty elegance of the interior. The hooded
fountain was the first of its kind and the ogival arches of the arcades an infrequent
elaboration. (Photo: Turkish Ministry of Tourism)

Plate 74 Selim II Complex, Payas, 1574. This large kervansaray with its spacious street market, mosque and college also includes an excellent example of an Ottoman castle. It consists of a powerful gatehouse and a walled enclosure in which the wooden barracks of the garrison were set. In the distance is an earlier Genoese stronghold. (Photo: G. Goodwin)

Plate 75 Selim II Mausoleum, Istanbul, 1577, tile panel.
Architect: Sinan. At this period, when a sultan died his offspring were executed to ensure the safety of his chosen successor, in this case Murat III. Five sons of the gentle and poetic sultan were executed when he fell fatally at the bath after drinking too much, as well he might when born to such an office. This panel adorns the porch wall. (Photo: W. Ball)

Plate 76 Kiliç Ali Pasha Complex, Istanbul, 1580. Architect: Sinan. This wealthy Grand Admiral was an Italian nobleman who was taken prisoner with his father. The heavy use of lead is symbolic of Sinan's later style. (Photo: G. Goodwin)

Plate 77 Zal Mahmut Pasha Complex, Istanbul, 1580. Architect: Sinan.
The variation in levels creates interest. Sinan had to incorporate two existing
medreses besides the cells of the upper court which is not rectangular because of the
irregular shape of the land. The lecture hall is therefore set on one side.
(Photo: G. Goodwin)

Plate 78 Muradiye Complex, Manisa, interior of mosque.
The appointments inside the mosque are very fine especially the late Iznik tiles. Murad III, whose mother was Venetian, was something of an aesthete. The sloping casements windows at roof level help to flood the interior with light. (Photo: Michael Stewart Thompson)

Plate 79 Muradiye Complex, Manisa, college. It is probable that Sinan only planned the mosque but the medrese is fine, although the kitchen block beyond is large but without architectural distinction. The college court is beautifully spacious and is a perfect example of the Ottoman style. (Photo: Turkish Ministry of Tourism)

Plate 80 Atık Valide Complex, Üsküdar. Sinan set his mihrabs in apses where panels of tiles flowered as if in a garden. This was a feature of early Ottoman architecture, introduced after the capture of Istanbul, that Sinan accepted with little modification. They thus form a link with Byzantine churches. (Photo: G. Goodwin)

Plate 81 Atık Valide Complex, Üsküdar, royal loge (hünkâr mahfile).
This royal loge was redecorated in the reign of Osman III with a notable trompe-l'oeil
panel. The lattice had already been added. The second portico of this mosque was also
a later addition. (Photo: Artomonov Collection, Freer Gallery of Art.)

Plate 82 Atık Valide Complex, Üsküdar, tile panel. Beautiful as the earlier
periods of Iznik tiles are, it is difficult not to regard the late 16th century as the
flowering of the art. This detail of the panel on the left of the apse of this mosque
represents the ideal garden of the Ottomans. (Photo: G. Goodwin)

**Plate 83 Kurşunlu (Leaded)
Mosque, Kayseri, 1585.**
Architect: probably Sinan, by proxy.
Sinan certainly did not return to his
old native province at this period.
The double portico is very fine as is
the ordering of the interior space.
The mosque is called Kurşunlu
because lead was sufficiently costly to
command prestige. (Photo: Michael
Stewart Thompson)

Plate 84 Mesih Pasha Mosque, Istanbul, 1585. Architect: possibly Sinan but more probably Davut Agha or Mehmet Agha. The galleries extend over flanking vestibules in a manner borrowed from Selimiye. The grillework lunettes are noteworthy. The eunuch builder was briefly Grand Vizer but was more notorious for his cruelty as Viceroy of Egypt. (Photo: Michael Stewart Thompson)

Plate 85 Topkapısaray, Istanbul, Orta Kapı or Middle Gate, 16th century. This is the gate to the present museum but was known as the middle gate since the outer precinct stretched to the Gate of Majesty opposite Hagia Sophia. In the tower, statesmen were incarcerated prior to their execution when they fell from favour, since slaves they were born and slaves they were even as adopted members of the Ottoman family. (Photo: J. Raby)

Plate 86 Topkapısaray, Istanbul, inscription over the Middle Gate. The gate
was embellished by the inscription of Murat III and restored by Mustafa III in the
18th century. His tughra or cypher incorporating his titles is an excellent example of
the elaborated form of the monogram dating from the earliest Turkish, nomad days.
(Photo: W. Ball)

Plate 87 Fountain and tomb of Sinan, Istanbul, 1588. Architect: Sinan. The tomb of the greatest Ottoman architect lies behind the fountain which brought trouble on his head because he tapped the royal water pipe in order to supply it. The wall has been rebuilt to enclose the Sinan family graveyard. His house or office lay beyond the tree. (Photo: G. Goodwin)

Plate 88 Takkeci Ibrahim Pasha Mosque, Istanbul, vestibule, 1592. The Hatmaker's mosque is largely built of wood and it is therefore all the more surprising to find it a museum of Iznik tiles of the most gorgeous kind. The dome and ceilings retain some of their original paintwork. (Photo: Artomonov Collection, Freer Gallery of Art)

Plate 89 Takkeci Ibrahim Pasha Mosque, Istanbul, tile. Vine panels are rare and this is a fine example of the design which would have been created by the artists attached to the palace and sent to Iznik for transfer to tile. It dates from the last quarter of the sixteenth century. (Photo: Turkish Ministry of Tourism)

Plate 90 Takkeci Ibrahim Pasha Mosque, Istanbul, tile detail. In contrast to the grandiose panels elsewhere in the mosque this small border tile is a masterpiece of simplicity consisting of three carnations and four tulips in a vase. (Photo: G. Goodwin)

Plate 91 Ahmediye (Blue Mosque) Complex, Istanbul, 1606–16. Architect:
Mehmet Agha. The complex included a large asylum now destroyed, a fine college,
now the Prime Ministerial archives, and a kitchen besides the mausoleum of the
young sultan and a fine kiosk. Ahmet I loved three things to excess – hunting,
women and God. (Photo: Turkish Ministry of Tourism)

Plate 92 Ahmediye Complex, Istanbul, minarets. The cost of this mosque bore heavily on the overtaxed rich who spread a malicious rumour that the six minarets were profane because they exceeded those of Mecca in number where there happened to be seven. The rumour still lives to mortify the soul of the voluptuous, God-fearing young sultan. (Photo: W. Ball)

Plate 93 Ahmediye Complex, Istanbul, mosque courtyard. Mehmet Agha integrated the height of the porticoes of the courtyard to an extent that diminishes the power of the colonnade before the mosque itself and encompasses the fine space of the open court with a certain monotony. The array of columns of equal dimensions, however, is fine. (Photo: W. Ball)

Plate 94 Ahmediye Complex, Istanbul, mosque interior. The dome is only 23.5 metres in diameter and 43 metres high, yet the supporting piers are massive if nicely facetted with Marmara marble. Neither the blue stencilling nor the glass is old or of any quality, but the tiles and bronzework are outstanding. (Photo: W. Ball)

Plate 95 Kara Mustafa Pasha of Merzifon Complex, Istanbul, completed after 1683. Architect: Hamdi Çavuş. The uncouth Grand Vizir was beheaded in Belgrade following a series of routs after his defeat before Vienna. His son with filial devotion completed the complex after his father's execution. (Photo: G. Goodwin)

Plate 96 Ali Pasha of Çorlu Complex, Istanbul, 1708. This small complex fills an irregular site with modest mosque, college and tomb in which the head of the decapitated Grand Vizir was deposited when brought back from Mytilene. He was a man of ability whose policies clashed with those of his master, Ahmet III. (Photo: G. Goodwin)

Plate 97 Ahmet III Library, Topkapısaray, Istanbul, 1719. The library replaced the Kiosk of the Pool whose fine columns were moved in front of the present Treasury. The library is not symmetrical which adds interest and beneath the portico is a handsome fountain. The lofty chamber makes an ideal reading room. (Photo: G. Goodwin)

Plate 98 Nevşehirli Ibrahim Pasha Mosque, Nevşehir, 1720. The style is still classical but with the fragility of a new elegance expressed by the eight slender turrets round the dome. Nevşehir, or the New Town, was planned by the pasha and has broad streets and open spaces laid out in a grid system. (Photo: Michael Stewart Thompson)

Plate 99 Ahmet III Fountain, Istanbul, 1738. 'With what a wall has Sultan Ahmet dammed the waters . . .' runs the inscription of Seyit Vehbi Efendi, a loquacious poet. It had four corner fountains from which water or sherbet iced with snow was given out in bronze cups and four spigots for filling ewers. (Photo: W. Ball)

Plate 100 Hacı Mehmet Emin Agha Fountain, Istanbul, 1741. The family graveyard lies behind the fine water kiosk. The provision of water was a great act of charity, above all in Istanbul where citizens continually tapped the pipes of state or religious foundations. The agha was a cavalry commander. (Photo: Michael Stewart Thompson)

Plate 101 Nuruosmaniye Complex, Istanbul, 1748–55. Architect: Çelebi
Mustafa Agha or, more probably, Simeon Kalfa. Mustafa was the figurehead and
Simeon the real builder of this, the first important building of the baroque period.
The dependencies include a college and elegant library grouped irregularly round an
outer precinct. (Photo: G. Goodwin)

Plate 102 Nuruosmaniye Complex, Istanbul, mosque courtyard. The horseshoe-shaped courtyard is unique and other baroque details include curved buttresses, shaven stalactites, and lofty portals. The prayer hall remains uncompromisingly square. (Photo: Turkish Ministry of Tourism).

Plate 103 Ayasma (Sacred Spring) Mosque, Üsküdar, 1757–60. The mosque was built by Mustafa III in honour of his mother. The interior is crowded and enriched by polychrome marble panels instead of tiles. The baroque pursuit of loftiness continued with this mosque and examples of charming stone dovecotes decorate the south wall. (Photo: G. Goodwin)

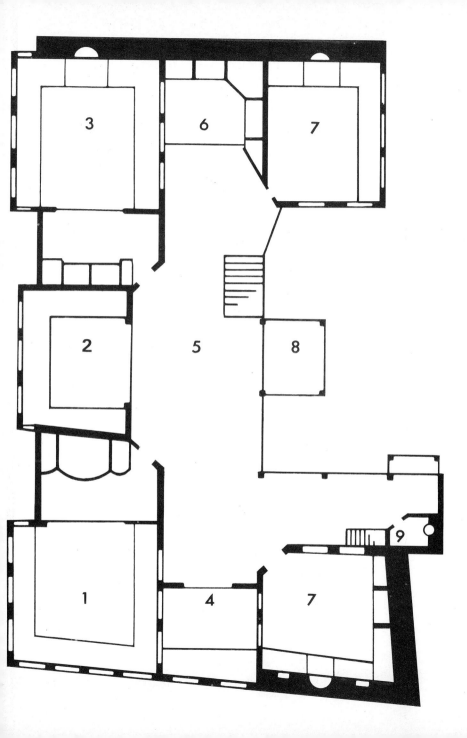

Fig. 14 Çakır Agha Konak, Birgi

1 Summer salon
2 Kiosk
3 Winter salon
4 and 6 Service areas
5 Verandah
7 Private chambers
8 Agha's bower
9 Closet

Plate 104 Çakır Agha Konak, Birgi, late 18th century. This very large mansion built of wood on stone foundations has a court extending to a terraced garden and is flanked by service rooms. The two upper storeys with their salons and retiring rooms possess grand verandahs for daily life and a bower with a throne for the agha. (Photo: Michael Stewart Thompson)

Plate 105 Çakır Agha Konak, Birgi, the summer saloon. This is a fine example of an Ottoman reception room with sofas used as beds at night. The lower casements have no glass but only shutters. The painting of Istanbul is a typical example of the lively naive art of the period. (Photo: Turkish Ministry of Tourism)

Plate 106 Çakır Agha Konak, a private chamber. The ocak or plaster chimneypiece is an example of baroque flimsiness taking over from the great classical bronze hoods. The doorway cuts across the corner of the room, a common feature of Ottoman homes and appears to invite the visitor into the room. (Photo: Michael Stewart Thompson)

Plate 107 Ishak Pasha Saray, Doğubayezit, about 1784. This immense palace of a local chieftain is built on a spur of the foothills of Mount Ararat in an astonishing revival of Georgian, Armenian and Seljuk architectural styles. The unhappy monuments have been looted, used as quarry and now patched up. (Photo: G. Goodwin)

Plate 108 Mirişah Sultan Complex, Eyüp, 1796. Truly lyrical in its pursuit of
curves, the charity is the work of the mother of Selim III who saw her son murdered.
The public kitchen supplies 500 poor dependents with a meal each day.
(Photo: Michael Stewart Thompson)

Plate 109 Izzet Pasha Mosque, Safranbolu, 1796. Good provincial mosques were built in the baroque style within the straight-jacket of square hall and hemispherical dome. Here the irregular site was used to create an angular court, now ruined by a crude fountain, dominated by the broad stairway up to the mosque itself. (Photo: G. Goodwin)

Plate 110 Market Han, Milas, 18th century. This is a typical merchants' lodging in a small country town. Largely built of wood the lodgings are set over the storerooms around the four sides of a courtyard. The gate was securely barred at night when a han became akin to a fortress. (Photo: G. Goodwin)

Plate 111 Sadullah Pasha Yalı (Mansion), Istanbul, late 18th century. The great wooden houses of the Bosphorus with their gardens, winter gardens and hillside parks are dwindling fast. Divided into harem or family apartments and selâmlik or reception rooms, their appendages include hamams and boathouses sometimes running in under the house. (Photo: G. Goodwin)

Plate 112 Sarfat Pasha Yalı, Istanbul, 18th century, now destroyed. The harem or private wing and the stone hamam had already been demolished but the loss of the state apartments in the fire of 1976 was a tragedy. Although yalıs were built of wood on a stone and brick foundation, some central halls were panelled in marble. (Photo: G. Goodwin)

Plate 113 Hasıp Pasha Yalı, Istanbul, early 19th century. This mansion is remarkable for its oval salon. It is cantilevered over the water in the manner that attracted Le Corbusier. It also attracted the ferryboat captains before the World Wars for it was their custom to sweep in low below the windows and hoot and wave at the ladies of the household. (Photo: G. Goodwin)

Plate 114 Selim III Mosque, Haydarpaşa, 1804. The poet and reformer, Selim III, built this mosque above the vast barracks of his new army, meant to replace the Janissary Corps, and they were used by Florence Nightingale during the Crimean War. The mosque is the last truly baroque monument. The minarets were rebuilt. (Photo: G. Goodwin)

Plate 115 Emir Sultan Complex, Bursa, 1804. The old mosque was rebuilt by Selim III but was again damaged in the earthquake of 1855 which brought down all the minarets of Bursa. The mosque remains square but the courtyard was transformed by the use of wood and gay paint over ogee arches. (Photo: G. Goodwin)

Plate 116 Nusretiye Mosque, Istanbul, 1826. Architect: Kirkor Balian. The victory mosque commemorates Mahmut II's triumph over the Janissaries. The minarets are the slenderest in Islam; over the porch are royal apartments and the courtyard lies beside the mosque, facing the sea. The architect was trained in Paris and the founder of a dynasty of Armenian royal architects. (Photo: Turkish Ministry of Tourism)

Plate 117 Yeni Köprü or Meriç Köprüsü, the New Bridge or Bridge over the Maritza River, Edirne, 1847. This bridge which was built by the Sultan Abdülmecid in the course of five years follows the old Ottoman tradition with a guard post and relieving arches in the Roman manner between the thirteen main arches that span the river. (Photo: Turkish Ministry of Tourism)

Plate 118 Hırkai Şerif Mosque, Istanbul, 1851. Built by Abdülmecid to house one of the two mantles of the Prophet, this flamboyant mosque is panelled with multi-coloured marbles and its furnishings are ornate. The calligraphy is the work of Mustafa Izzet Efendi and the gifted sultan himself. (Photo: G. Goodwin)

Plate 119 Tombstones, Süleymaniye, Istanbul, 19th century. Ottoman tombstones possess considerable charm. Those over the graves of women are carved with flowers while men's headstones wore the turban, and later the fez, according to their rank. Little tombstones mark the graves of children. (Photo: G. Goodwin)

Plate 120 Dolmabahçe Palace, Istanbul, 1853. Architect: Karabet Balian.
The three sections of the palace were each based in plan on that of the Çinili Kiosk.
There is a fine esplanade beside the water, a clock tower and the mosque of the
Queen Mother, Bezmialem. The chandeliers and scagliola work are particular
features. (Photo: Turkish Ministry of Tourism)

Plate 121 Houses, Amasya, various periods. Earthquakes have destroyed much of what was once one of the most splendid wooden towns of Anatolia, ranking with Safranbolu, but the line of konaks beside the river survive still projecting over the water below the citadel which made Amasya so important. (Photo: Michael Stewart Thompson)

Plate 122 Houses, Amasya, 19th century. With the rock tombs of the Hellenistic period above them impervious to the centuries, these mansions are too frail to last much longer. Moreover, they are exceptionally spacious and take their ease along the river bank. (Photo: G. Goodwin)

Plate 123 Konaks, Plovdiv, 19th century. The Ottoman presence in the provinces of Europe and the Near East is marked by the mansions of the local officials and those of Plovdiv are particularly carefully preserved. This governor's mansion is spacious and set in a pretty garden. (Photo: G. Goodwin)

Plate 124 Turkish Konak, Plovdiv, 19th century. Not all the Ottoman houses in the provinces were as grand as that of the governor with its vast central salon, but the policy of careful restoration pursued in Bulgaria reveals the charm and character of smaller houses as well as great. (Photo: G. Goodwin)

Plate 125 Safranbolu, 19th century mansions. The town is built on spurs of hills above the Black Sea plain. It was therefore easy to divide into the government quarter seen here, the Turkish and the Greek quarters. Each is remarkable for the fine mansions and their gardens that take care not to obscure their neighbour's view. (Photo: G. Goodwin)

Plate 126 Gate to the University, formerly the Ministry of War, about 1866. Architect: F. Bourgeois or subordinate. This building stands where once the delightful baroque canopied porch in the Ottoman baroque style flourished. It is a vulgar imitation of the Moorish and may serve to illustrate the unfortunate intrusion of aliens into a world beyond their imaginings. It serves as the faculty club. (Photo: W. Ball)

Plate 127 Abdülaziz Mosque, Konya, 1872. The Balian style was not popular in the provinces but this mosque is an exception. The use of a hood over the minaret balconies was the antipathy of the classical Ottoman style. For all its large windows and ornateness, the mosque remains a domed square. (Photo: G. Goodwin)

Plate 128 Tree, Milas–Bodrum road. Saints are often buried under old trees beside a road where their shade serves as a wayside shrine for ritual prayers. Superstitions far older than Islam result in the flying of coloured rags to attract the attention of the Immortals from whom favours are demanded.

Plate 129 Kara Mustafa Pasha Mosque, Merzifon, paintwork inside wooden dome over the fountain, 1875. This scene is typical of popular Turkish art in the 19th century which can still be found both in public and private buildings. It is a tradition which continues with the decorating of peasant carts at Sivas, Inegöl and elsewhere and also the handcarts of street vendors. (Photo: Michael Stewart Thompson)

Plate 130 Galata from the Bridge, Istanbul, 19th century. The bridge was erected by German engineers at the turn of the century and the iron balustrade is a copy of the old patterns once wrought in stone. Foreign influence is reflected in the Genoese style of the Banco da Roma but an Islamic love of calligraphy is seen in the signwriting in the sky. (Photo: G. Goodwin)